Physical Characteristics of the Rottweiler

(from the American Kennel Club breed standard)

Body: The chest is roomy, broad and deep, reaching to elbow, with well pronounced forechest and well sprung, oval ribs. Back is straight and strong. Loin is short, deep and well muscled. Croup is broad, of medium length and only slightly sloping.

Tail: Docked short, close to body, leaving one or two tail vertebrae.

Hindquarters: Upper thigh is fairly long, very broad and well muscled. Stifle joint is well turned. Lower thigh is long, broad and powerful. Feet are somewhat longer than the front feet.

Coat: Outer coat is straight, coarse, dense, of medium length and lying flat.

Color: Always black with rust to mahogany markings. The demarcation between black and rust is to be clearly defined.

Size: Dogs—24 inches to 27 inches. Bitches—22 inches to 25 inches, with preferred size being mid-range of each sex.

Rottweiler

◇

by William Jonas

Contents

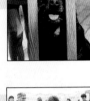

KENNEL CLUB BOOKS: ROTTWEILER
ISBN: 1-59378-203-9

Copyright © 1998 • Revised American Edition: Copyright © 2003
Kennel Club Books, Inc., 308 Main Street, Allenhurst, NJ 07711 USA
Cover Design Patented: US 6,435,559 B2 • Printed in South Korea

PHOTOS BY:
Norvia Behling, Carolina Biological Supply, Liza Clancy, Doskocil, Isabelle Français, James Hayden-Yoav, James R. Hayden, RBP, Carol Ann Johnson, Bill Jonas, Dwight R. Kuhn, Dr. Dennis Kunkel, Nancy Liguori, Mikki Pet Products, Phototake, Jean Claude Revy, Alice Roche and C. James Webb.

Illustrations by Renée Low.

The Rottweiler's unique coloration and high level of trainability have made the breed one of the world's most recognizable and popular.

History of the Rottweiler

No matter how long I am owned by Rottweilers, I will always be fascinated by the unique rust markings over every dog's eyes and on the cheeks. I have been an impassioned student of the breed, its breeding, pedigrees, genetics and history, and still I am fascinated. In Australia, as I learned on a visit there, the eye marks are called "pips," a charming and typically Aussie name for these marks! I know that many other breeds have distinctive color markings, but the Rottweiler stands out among the crowd, especially since he stands so tall and proud, as befits his remarkable German heritage.

It is my wish that this introduction to the Rottweiler breed could begin with a definitive statement to show the genesis of the breed. I wish I could pinpoint one breeder (of course in the small town of Rottweil, Germany) who created the breed and show the beginning Rottweiler owner exactly how this great breed began—perhaps

Rottweilers are great herding dogs and are used by many sheep and cattle farmers.

Rottweilers all over the world have the same basic appearance. This is a German-bred dog.

chosen canine was said to be a protective dog that also possessed herding abilities—a description that well suits our Rottweiler. The Romans occupied Germany for no less than two centuries, and their established city there was called *das Rote Wil*, from which the breed's current name derives. Further crediting this theory, early historians cite that direct descendants of the breed lived in areas of Germany that were accessible to the roads built by the Germans in that period.

That said, it is evident that the Romans did not arrive with the handsome black-and-mahogany guard dog we know today, though it is probable the even explaining how the pips were born—but it is not possible. As with most other breeds that have been around for more than a century, the exact origins are not known.

THE BREED IN THE FATHERLAND

Most historians trace the Rottweiler back to the invasion of Germany by the Romans who crossed the Alps during the first century A.D. Whether the dogs the Romans used were the ancestors of today's Rottweiler cannot be definitely known, though their

PLANNED MATINGS

It was only in the 19th century that humans really took notice of the dogs around them, and how they looked, what color they were and how large they were. Dogs all along have been helpmates—some dogs hunted, some dogs killed vermin and some dogs protected the property. No one bred the big black dog to the big black bitch because they were both black and big, necessarily. More than likely, humans paired dogs for their abilities. To produce a strong, protective dog, they would mate two dogs with those desirable qualities. Thus were progenerated various dogs with superior abilities.

mastiff-type dog they employed, combined with existing dogs in Germany during the first few centuries A.D., formed the basis of today's Rottweiler. That the Romans venerated the mastiff-type dogs, known as Molossus, is well documented. *Cave canum* (beware of the dog) is an ancient Latin saying that was posted anywhere the Molossus dwelled. Much like today, similar signs are posted. My favorite, which I have seen around town, shows the silhouette of a Rottweiler and reads, "I can make it to the gate in three seconds, can you?" Surely a daunting thought for a would-be intruder! The Romans employed these mastiffs for protection and military work as well as the popular sport of dog fighting. More than one of the Rottweiler's ancestors were lost in the famous Colosseum in Rome; today only the shell of the great arena stands as a reminder of the potential cruelty of humankind to animals and to one another.

Also important to ancient Rome were the drover dogs, dogs

The Rottweiler's markings are one of the breed's defining characteristics. Look at the similarity between these three dogs.

This action shot shows some of the problems with which Rottweilers have to deal. Rottweilers, while very strict disciplinarians with their flocks, rarely injure the animals left in their trust.

used to drive cattle over long distances. The Rottweiler's ancestors are believed to have been employed by Julius Caesar, one of Rome's great emperors. It was Caesar's notion that his armies should have fresh meat to eat, instead of the traditional salted portions. The method whereby his soldiers found their ration of meatballs and bracciole was to have the cattle go to the men on hoof, thus requiring a strong dog to maneuver the livestock with skill, grace and speed. The droving abilities of the Rottweiler, even today, speak well of these dogs' innate skill.

During the eighth century A.D., the city of Rottweil, Germany was born. The word *Rote* (as in *das Rote Wil*) referred to the red coloration of the tiles and bricks that were used in the construction of the city. These red tiles were dug up from buildings that collapsed, dating back to the Roman occupation of Germany some 500 years prior. The city of Rottweil was exceptional for the high esteem with which it held its dog, in a time when Germans did not consider dogs much more than tools and helpers.

As a helper in Rottweil, the breed became known as a

Rottweilers enjoy playing with kids... and kids' toys! Be careful, though, as children's toys are not made to withstand a Rottie's strong teeth and jaws.

The city of
Rottweil, Germany
is credited as the
basis for the name
of the Rottweiler.
A citizen of
Rottweil is also
called a Rottweiler
in both English and
German.

butcher's dog, or, in German,
Metzgerhund, driving cattle to
and from market, the very trait
that Caesar employed for the
Roman armies. The dogs were
tough, fearless and tireless, and
rarely backed down from a
confrontation with a bull or
another dog. Dog fights among
these butcher's dogs became
somewhat common, and any dog
with a record of biting had to be
muzzled.

SWISS COUSINS

The Rottweiler likely has close cousins
in Switzerland. It is believed that many
of the Italian mastiffs, *en route* to
Germany, were left in Switzerland as
they crossed the Alps. The Greater
Swiss Mountain Dog is a smooth-
coated black dog, a bit taller and with
different pips. Its three Swiss brethren
include the Bernese Mountain Dog,
Appenzeller and Entelbucher.

A POPULARITY JOLT

Who could imagine that a breed beginning the 20th century with such a shoddy representation would finish the century as one of the world's most popular dogs? Never before has such a large and powerful dog become so unbelievably popular around the world. In the U.S., the Rottweiler climbed the ranks to become the number-two dog in the country (in terms of annual registrations as recorded by the AKC). The breed actually overcame such long-standing popular companion dogs as the Golden Retriever, German Shepherd Dog and Poodle!

The breed's decline was instigated by the government's outlawing of cattle droving, whereby the more industrialized society was finding other methods of moving livestock with wagons and mules.

Additionally, the threat of wild animals, such as bears and boars, had nearly disappeared. By and large, the Rottweiler was "down-sized" (in modern-day terminology) and the breed nearly fell into extinction. Concerned German dog lovers rescued the breed, which had dwindled down to one dog in Rottweil by the year 1905.

When the Deutscher Rottweiler Klub (DRK) was

Breed representatives from different countries—here is a German-bred Rottweiler, while the facing page shows an English-bred dog.

A beautifully proportioned and marked Rottweiler, showing great strength and nobility.

formed in the year 1907, it was the first breed club for the Rottweiler in Germany. As dog politics are no smoother than government politics, a second club was formed the very same year called the International Rottweiler Klub (IRK). Just 12 years later a third club, the South German Rottweiler Club, was created, and confusion and cantankerous politics reigned. Fortunately, for both German Rottweiler owners and students of the breed, the DRK and IRK did the sensible thing and combined to form the Allgemeiner Deutscher Rottweiler Klub (ADRK) in 1921, which absorbed the South German club within three short years.

While it was advantageous to have only one club in Germany, and therefore one stud book to refer to, the Rottweilers already were varying in type, some with weaker heads. Greater uniformity of conformation and sounder construction became the unanimous goal of the new club, and the breed was soon appearing more consistent with superior temperaments and work abilities. The club did not sacrifice type,

keeping in mind the original droving dogs and their traits. It should be noted that the ADRK made a conscious decision regarding the color desirable for the Rottweiler. While the black and rust coloration was predominant, there were other colors as well, including tan and beige, plus some white markings. The selection of the black and rust coloration by the ADRK meant that only dogs of the desirable coloration would be approved for breeding.

Since cattle droving had become nonexistent for the breed, new employment was required. This brought about the beginning of Schutzhund in 1930. This working degree tested the dog's protective abilities, intelligence and obedience. It became the desired litmus test for breeding stock in Germany and a requirement for Rottweilers to become champions. In addition to attack training, Schutzhund also embraces tracking, basic obedience, the dog's steadiness and willingness to obey commands.

The ADRK standard for the Rottweiler was first adopted in Germany during the early part of the 20th century; it has remained virtually unaltered over the years, speaking highly of the consistency of the Rottweiler's conformation and temperament.

THE FIRST STANDARD
The first standard drafted for the Rottweiler occurred in 1901. This description was a joint standard for the Rottweiler and Leonberger.

THE ROTTWEILER IN THE U.K.

The first Rottweiler to enter Great Britain did so in 1936, imported by fancier Thelma Gray. The first bitch was named Diana v.d. Amalienburg, SchH. I, whom Mrs. Gray sold to Mrs. Simmons of the to be a well-trained working dog. Anna is believed to have been the only Rottweiler left in England when World War II was ended.

Mrs. Gray imported three other dogs before the war—Asta

Steadiness, obedience and bravery are required in every well-bred Rottweiler.

Crowsteps prefix. The second Rottweiler, also a bitch, was Enne v. Pfalzgau, a good winning three-year-old German dog, bred by Herr Weinmann. She was said to have a weak head that she passed to her progeny. She was sold to Miss Paton, and her first litter was lost due to distemper except one pup, Anna from Rozavel, who grew up von Norden, Arnold v.d. Eichener and Vefa von Kohlerwald—some of which did well at the shows but were sent to Ireland during the war and were never seen again. Miss Homan imported Benno von Kohlerwald, who did not do well in quarantine and had a shaky temperament once released, and was sent to the Air

Through importation of dogs from Germany, Holland and Sweden, and through careful breeding, the quality of Rottweilers in the U.K. steadily improved.

Force for use during the war.

The real beginning of the breed in England is marked by the end of the war, since the ten years prior to the war's ending did not amount to even a breeding pair of Rottweilers in England. Anna was the only bitch in the U.K., and by 1945 she was nine years old and hardly in breeding condition. She retired as a pet quite happily.

While serving in Germany as a veterinary officer, Captain Roy-Smith admired the Rottweiler, which he encountered many times while in the military. This young vet was the first to import a Rottweiler into the U.K. after the war. Although there are reports of Rottweilers in Britain as early as 1913, no dogs were registered with The Kennel Club when Captain Roy-Smith inquired. The Rottweilers that Roy-Smith imported as well as the foundation dogs imported by Mrs. Joanna Chadwick formed an important basis for the breed in Britain. These first Rottweilers came to England almost exclusively from Germany, and later from Holland and Sweden, where the breed had established a stronghold. Among the British kennels that imported Rottweilers in the 1950s and '60s were Rintelna, Mallion, Blackforest, Gamegards and Taucas.

The Rottweiler Club in the U.K. was established in 1960 by Mrs. M. Wait with an original membership of 25 Rottweiler fanciers, with Mrs. Gray serving as the first president, befitting her early efforts with the breed

Post-War Dogs Imported into England

Dog	Breeder	Date whelped	Importer
Berny v. Weyher	Carl Voigt	June 11, 1952	Capt. Roy-Smith
Ajax v. Fuhrenkamp	Wilhelm Drevenstedt	April 20, 1952	Capt. Roy-Smith
Wuinta Eulenspiegel	Marieanne Bruns	February 28, 1954	Mrs. Joanna Chadwick
Rudi Eulenspiegel	Marieanne Bruns	May 21, 1954	Mrs. Joanna Chadwick
Rintelna Lotte v. Osterberg	?	February 1952	Capt. Roy-Smith
Bim Eulenspiegel	Marieanne Bruns	May 19, 1958	Mrs. Joanna Chadwick & Mr. Newton
Vera v. Filstalstrand	?	?	Capt. Roy-Smith & Mary Macphail

in the U.K. The second club, known as the British Rottweiler Association, was also formed shortly thereafter, and the two clubs, surprisingly, cooperate well with one another.

By the late 1960s, the Rottweiler qualified for Challenge Certificates at Championship Shows of The Kennel Club. The first champion was made up in 1966, a bitch by the name of Chesara Dark Destiny, owned by Pat Lanz.

THE ROTTWEILER IN THE U.S.
The 1930s marked the first Rottweilers to be registered with the American Kennel Club (AKC), beginning with a German-bred bitch named Stina v. Felsenmeer, owned by August Knecht. The first litter bred in the U.S. was accomplished by Otto Denny in September 1930. AKC recognition of the breed was achieved in 1931, with very few Rottweilers in the country and no standard accepted. Knecht and Denny mated their dogs to produce the first AKC-registered litter. Other litters were registered with the AKC over the next couple of decades, mainly by German immigrants who had been Rottweiler breeders in the Fatherland.

The first champion to earn that title in 1948, Zero was owned and bred by Noel P. Jones. His litter sister Zola became the second champion, owned by Erna Pinkerton. Jones later handled Ch. Kurt to a Group One, the first Working Group to be claimed by a Rottweiler. The breed became more known as an obedience titleist than a conformation show champion, with Ch. Zada's Zenda, CD becoming the first Rottweiler to win an obedience title. Gero v. Rabenhorst, an important import, qualified for

HEALTH FOUNDATION
Founded in 1998 by the American Rottweiler Club (ARC), the Rottweiler Health Foundation is a non-profit, completely volunteer organization designed to improve the overall health status of the breed. The Foundation raises funds through donations and membership dues and has individual members as well as member clubs. Among the stated goals are the fostering and promotion of education about canine health, including life-threatening diseases and hereditary conditions; the dissemination of information about the breed's health and proper care, including a national database of resources; and indentifying the major diseases and the reliable researchers for each.

CD, CDX and UD, the first three progressive titles in AKC obedience trials. This accomplishment in 1941 marked the first Rottweiler to reach the UD title.

Laura Coonley was the first person to breed an American Best in Show (BIS) Rottweiler. The dog was Ch. Kato v. Donnaj, CDX, TD, owned by Jan Marshall. Kato did not enjoy the distinction of the only BIS Rottweiler for very long, as his own brother, Ch. Rodsden's Duke Du Trier, swept the victory the very next day. It was May 1971. Duke repeated his victory in Canada, becoming the first Rottweiler to win BIS in that country.

While the Rottweiler has had five important breed clubs in the U.S., the American Rottweiler Club, established in 1971, is the official parent club. Among the other clubs are the Colonial Rottweiler Club, the Medallion Rottweiler Club and the Golden State Rottweiler Club. Each club is a separate entity, though each club stands for the betterment of the breed and the protection of the breed standard in the U.S.

Few breeds have excelled in the U.S. like the Rottweiler. The 1990s were colored in black and tan, and the Rottweiler reigned as one of the nation's most popular breeds. Only out-registered by the Labrador Retriever, the Rottweiler rode out the 1990s with numbers exceeding hundreds of thousands of dogs.

This noble German breed has attracted many an admirer in the United States.

Characteristics of the Rottweiler

Unlike the other breeds that have heralded top ranks in popularity, the Rottweiler is neither a sweet hunting dog (like the Labrador Retriever, Golden Retriever or Cocker Spaniel) nor an adoring shepherd type (like the German Shepherd Dog). Neither does he have any similarity to the Poodle, other than the affection of the German people for both breeds. No, the Rottweiler is a massive, hard-working dog whose weight can exceed 100 pounds and whose height can be up to 27 inches at the shoulder. Surely, the Rottweiler must possess many fine attributes to endear him to the likes of so many dog owners around the world.

The Rottweiler's strength and courage earned him favor early in the 20th century. After suffering great neglect in the early 1900s, the breed was "drafted" into service in World War I. The breed's performance for the Axis powers proved its superior abilities as a military dog, thus the Rottweiler's outstanding performance in Schutzhund decades later. Living in today's society,

The Rottweiler is as popular as a family pet as he is for guard and protection work.

Although derived from Roman Molossers, the Rottweiler bears little resemblance to the Neapolitan Mastiff, shown here.

with a high crime rate in both cities and smaller towns, a guard dog with impressive size and ability to match is greatly in demand, and the Rottweiler remains one of the top choices for the job.

PHYSICAL CHARACTERISTICS

Unlike other mastiff breeds, such as the Neapolitan Mastiff, the Dogue de Bordeaux and the Bullmastiff, the Rottweiler is a handsome dog—balanced, well proportioned and not exaggerated like the aforementioned giants that suffer from acromegaly and worse conditions. It is even fair to say that for the Rottweiler's size, he is a very healthy dog, suffering only from hip dysplasia and a few other conditions, and his lifespan is greater than other dogs his size. The Rottweiler's sleek black coat, accented by his perfectly placed mahogany markings, cuts a handsome figure. His head is impres-

sive but not so massive that it is out of proportion with his body. He is, by all counts, a majestic animal of considerable size, though he is not as giant as the Mastiff and the others.

PERSONALITY

A major attribute that the Rottweiler possesses in spades is his trainability. This is a most intelligent and obedient dog, capable of learning a multitude of tasks. His history as a droving dog, military and protection dog and obedience and show dog speaks well of the Rottweiler's diversity and versatility.

AN ACTIVE BREED

Given the many talents of the Rottweiler, as his history as a drover dog, protection dog, military dog, etc., has conveyed, you must find outlets for your Rottweiler's abilities. You cannot leave your Rottweiler alone in the yard for hours without supervision or, worse, tied to a post to run in circles of boredom until you decide to check on him. No, Rottweilers are creative, intelligent creatures that need activities. Whether it is a run on the beach every evening, a jog through the park in the morning or a full-blown itinerary of challenging events, your Rottweiler will be grateful. Some of the kinds of events that inventive Rottweiler owners enjoy with their dogs include obedience trials, agility trials, tracking, herding tests and more.

The Rottweiler is a naturally protective animal with the strength to back up his protective instincts. Many trainers advise undertaking the Rottweiler's education with great caution, given the natural instincts and strength of this dog. Schutzhund training has been used with great success when executed by professional handlers in a controlled environment. Novices should not even consider attempting to sleeve train (i.e., attack train) the Rottweiler. Professional assistance is a must. In Germany, there are countless experienced, expert Schutzhund trainers; in the U.S., it is more difficult to secure the services of such qualified professionals and, therefore, extreme caution is advised when considering this type of training.

The Rottweiler is trustworthy and confident, befitting his stature and his proud German upbringing. There are stories about Rottweilers' being employed as "moneyholders" for trade, with a money bag tied around the Rottweiler's neck. Trust and strength go paw in paw with the Rottweiler.

The German standard for the Rottweiler, as accepted by the ADRK, well describes the ideal character of the breed: "His figure, which is short, compact, and strong in proportion, gives every indication not only of high intelligence but also of wonderful devotion, eagerness and joy in work. A tractable dog with considerable power and stubborn endurance. His general appearance immediately proclaims him to be of deter-

Rottweilers are so popular because they are so versatile. They are family dogs, working dogs, guard dogs and tracking dogs, to name but a few.

mination and courage; his calm glance indicates his good humor and his unswerving fidelity. His nature exhibits no traces of disquietude, hastiness or indecision. Treachery, malice and falseness are entirely foreign to his nature."

Certainly the German standard describes a dog that goes far to impress many dog lovers: the qualities of fidelity, good humor and decisiveness are welcome in a dog of the Rottweiler's size and power. The Rottweiler is at once friendly and imposing. He does not make friends without reservations: a stranger is a stranger, not like the retrievers who accept everyone immediately as a close friend. Rottweilers are discerning, as their intelligence and good judgment allow. Their protective nature underscores this judgment as well, but once a Rottweiler has accepted you as a friend, you can be sure that you have a buddy to rely upon.

Rottweilers are ideal as protectors of family and property. The breed accepts each member of the family and is equally protective of father as he is of the smallest child. Rottweilers do not usually play favorites, though there are exceptions to every rule. We once owned a bitch that was extremely fond of my oldest son and had less devotion to the girls of our family. Nonetheless, the daughters of that bitch were affectionate and protective of all members of our family. Rottweilers tend to be individualistic—again, because they are smart and discerning creatures.

This intelligence does affect their trainability. As is commonly said of cats, they are too smart to proceed with constant repetition of a command. Once they have executed a command once or twice to your liking, they will likely tire of the "game" and look for a better outlet. "Why do humans persist in doing these silly exercises so many times? I got it the first time and it wasn't that exciting," thinks the Rottweiler. Some Rottweilers need more prompting than others, and

SCHUTZHUND

In Schutzhund trials, dogs are rated by performance and can earn the titles of SchH. I (beginner), SchH. II (intermediate) and SchH. III (master). These titles can be appended to the dog's name and pedigree.

patience is required when training a dog, no matter the breed.

If you have children in your home and are considering a Rottweiler, there are matters to be considered. A well-bred Rottweiler reared in a family with love and fairness is as trustworthy with children as the best of dogs. Given the Rottweiler's size and strength, however, many parents may choose not to take a chance. This is every parent's prerogative, but accidents and dog bites can happen with any breed. Actually, there are far more instances of Cocker Spaniels' biting children than any breed, including Rottweilers and Pit Bull Terriers. Any dog can do harm with his bite, regardless of size, and larger dogs tend to bite less intensely since they are confident about their strength. If you know the breeder of your dog and have discussed the temperament of dogs in that line, you should have faith in the Rottweiler that you purchase. Of course, caution is the rule, and you must never allow the Rottweiler to get the upper hand, whether the dog is dealing with the biggest man in the house or the smallest toddler. Dogs like to have positive examples to follow or else they try to become leaders. Their pack instinct enforces their need to have a leader—that leader must be you, followed by each member of your family. The Rottweiler must understand that he has the lowest rank in the household.

Are you well suited, indeed worthy, to own a Rottweiler? Have you the physical stamina to keep up with such a dog? Have you a fenced yard to provide ample exercise? Do you have the time to give a dog whose dedication and protectiveness are centered around you?

Not everyone is fit to own a Rottweiler. That much is obvious. You must not be hasty in deciding that this dog is for you and your home and family. Every dog deserves a fair shot and the best possible living situation possible. The Rottweiler needs a confident, competent owner who under-stands his needs and is able to provide properly for him.

Schutzhund, carting, herding tests, backpacking and camping, therapy-dog visits and public demonstrations are just some of the Rottie's favorite activities. Your time with your Rottweiler is only limited by your imagination,

A well-trained Rottweiler will accept children and other pets and still be protective against strangers and intruders.

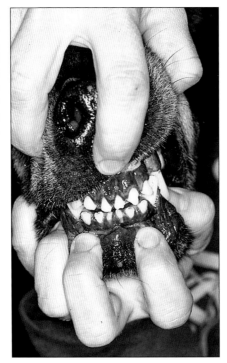

Rottweilers should have well-formed teeth. Brushing and regular dental exams will keep them that way for the life of the dog.

time and budget. Certainly your Rottweiler is the kind of dog who likes to try anything once. Since the breed has such a high level of trust for his human counterparts, Rottweilers will follow their owners to the ends of the earth!

HEALTH CONSIDERATIONS FOR THE ROTTWEILER

Rottweilers are generally healthy, active dogs. Advances in veterinary medicine, just as in human medicine, result in increased lifespans, but in our pets this has not proven to be a reliable hypothesis. Rottweilers reach their senior years at around seven years old,

which seems considerably young to us humans who do not retire until 55 or 65! In order to ensure our Rottweilers the longest possible lives, and the healthiest ones, we must be informed and provide our pets with the best health care possible.

This begins, of course, with visits to the vet and a proper schedule of vaccinations. Back in the late 1970s, a fatal disease known as parvovirus was first recorded. While it is a manageable disease today, without proper vaccinations, early diagnosis and prompt treatment, it can be deadly. Many prominent breeders throughout the 1980s and '90s lost valuable puppies to this dreaded disease. Your veterinarian will inform you of the best inoculation schedule, which usually begins at around eight weeks of age and is repeated every few weeks until around four months, and then followed up every six months until two years. Research has indicated that Rottweilers' immune systems are weaker than those of other breeds, so absolute

BIGGER'S NOT BETTER

When searching for a Rottweiler, owners are well advised to not seek out dogs that are bigger than the standard describes. These dogs will more likely suffer from joint problems and other conditions that accompany overbreeding and oversized dogs.

care is required to protect the breed from parvovirus, to which it seems unfortunately very susceptible.

As with most large breeds of dog, hip and elbow dysplasia have taken their toll on the Rottweiler breed. Hip dysplasia (HD), first recognized as a major problem in German Shepherd Dogs, has crippled (or badly deformed) many Rottweilers. Hip dysplasia in its most severe form can render a dog totally crippled. Since it is a hereditary condition, no Rottweiler who tests positive for hip dysplasia should be bred. While the incidence of hip dysplasia has been reduced since the 1970s when it was around 30%, today approximately 20% of Rottweilers test positive for the disease. Still worse, the incidence of elbow dysplasia (ED) in Rottweilers is upsettingly high,

with the percentage around 40 to 50%, and higher in males than females. Responsible breeders must test for both forms of dysplasia before breeding their dogs. Years ago, certain dysplastic champions were still extensively bred and therefore the number of puppies born with dysplasia was disturbingly high. Today, breeders exclude such dogs from their programs, regardless of their other virtues.

Discuss hip dysplasia and elbow dysplasia with your breeder. This is your best way to determine how cognizant of the problem the breeder is. A number of breeders propose that environmental factors also affect dysplasia in Rottweilers. Breeders who do not use non-slip matting in their whelping boxes may aggravate the potential condition. As puppies try to take their first steps

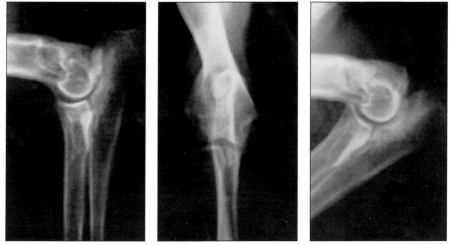

Elbow dysplasia in a three-and-a-half-year-old dog.

Photo courtesy of Dr. M. A. Stevenson, DVM, and the Journal of the American Veterinary Medicine Association.

and begin to slide around on the hard slippery surface of the whelping pen, their fragile ligaments and bones can be badly stressed. Since both types of dysplasia occur when the Rottweiler is fairly young (before 24 months for HD, before 7 months for ED), such a theory is believable. Other breeders propose that the diet of the puppy can affect the development of dysplasia and other cartilage diseases like osteochondrosis in susceptible dogs. Diets that are high in calcium, protein and fats should be discouraged, since Rottweilers are fast-growing dogs with the potential of putting too much weight too fast on their growing frames. Let's not rule out exercise from the picture—young Rottweilers should not be permitted to roughhouse and jump about wildly in play, since such unregulated exercise can result in cartilage tears and other injuries that may increase the risk of problems with osteochondrosis, HD or ED.

Another problem that is related to Rottweilers is known as bloat, sometimes referred to as gastric volvulus or gastric dilatation. Deep-chested large dogs are the most susceptible to this condition, characterized by the stomach's being distended with air, which is swallowed by the dog. Generally this is not a problem with puppies but with adults or older dogs. Dogs who tend to wolf

DO YOU KNOW ABOUT HIP DYSPLASIA?

Hip dysplasia is a fairly common condition found in Rottweilers, as well as other large breeds. When a dog has hip dysplasia, his hind leg has an incorrectly formed hip joint. By constant use of the hip joint, it becomes more and more loose, wears abnormally and may become arthritic.

Hip dysplasia can only be confirmed with an x-ray, but certain symptoms may indicate a problem. Your Rottweiler may have a hip dysplasia problem if he walks in a peculiar manner, hops instead of smoothly running, uses his hind legs in unison (to keep the pressure off the weak joint), has trouble getting up from a prone position and sits with both legs together on one side of his body.

As the dog matures, he may adapt well to life with a bad hip, but in a few years the arthritis develops and many Rottweilers with hip dysplasia become crippled.

Hip dysplasia is considered an inherited disease and can usually be diagnosed when the dog is up to two years old. Some experts claim that a special diet might help your puppy outgrow the bad hip, but the usual treatments are surgical—the removal of the pectineus muscle, the removal of the round part of the femur, reconstructing the pelvis or replacing the hip with an artificial one. All of these surgical interventions are expensive, but they are usually very successful. Follow the advice of your veterinarian.

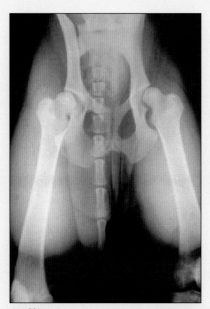

Good hips.

Compare the two hip joints and you'll understand dysplasia. Hip dysplasia is a badly worn hip joint caused by improper fit of the bone into the socket. It is easily the most common hip problem in Rottweilers.

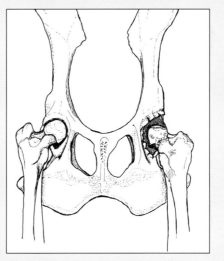

The healthy hip joint on the left and the unhealthy hip joint on the right.

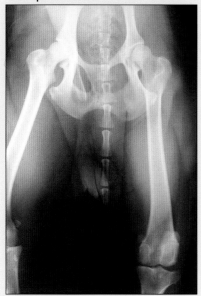

Moderate dysplasia.

ALL HE CAN BE
The behavior and personality of your Rottweiler will reflect your care and training more than any breed characteristics or indications. Remember that these dogs require a purposeful existence and plan your relationship around activities that serve this most basic and important need. All the good potential of the breed will necessarily follow.

their food and water, who run and play very vigorously or who are stressed by other factors are candidates for bloat. In the worst-case scenario, a dog whose stomach has bloated will die from the stomach's twisting, which stops the flow of food to the organ as well as the blood supply. Unfortu-

nately, about one-third of the dogs who suffer from this condition will die, though *immediate* veterinary assistance can prevent death. Many vets and breeders make recommendations to Rottweiler owners to help prevent the possible onset of bloat.

Since Rottweilers tend to love mealtime, their excitement can result in their gulping or wolfing their food. You want to discourage this as much as possible. Feed smaller meals two or three times a day. You can try placing large balls or chew toys in the bowl so that your dog has to eat around them. Only serve dry food after saturating it in water. Use bowl stands to elevate the dog's food. Take away the dog's fresh water at mealtimes, but leave it available throughout the day. Do not leave your dog's food sitting around all day. Offer it only at the designated mealtimes, and pick it up as soon as the dog walks away from the bowl. Schedule exercise times so that there is at least 90 minutes before and after each meal. These simple suggestions can mean the difference between life and death for your black-and-tan friend. It is but a small price to pay for all your Rottweiler gives you in terms of companionship, protection and amusement!

Other conditions that you may want to discuss with your vet include hypothyroidism, the most frequently seen hormonal condi-

You want your Rottweiler to stay healthy and active; practice preventative medicine and be proactive in his care.

tion in Rottweilers; osteochondrosis, a condition seen in young dogs that affects the cartilage; aortic stenosis, a congenital defect of the heart; degenerative myelopathy, affecting the spinal cord; progressive retinal atrophy and retinal dysplasia, congenital disorders of the retina that can result in blindness; and von Willebrand's disease, the most common congenital disease of the blood, affecting the clotting factor.

While this list may seem daunting to the new Rottweiler enthusiast, we present it here not to discourage your interest in our great breed, but instead to promote your responsible selection and husbandry of these truly worthy animals. Surely the list of diseases seen in humans would be as disheartening! Be a responsible owner, be informed and enjoy the longest possible life with your Rottweiler.

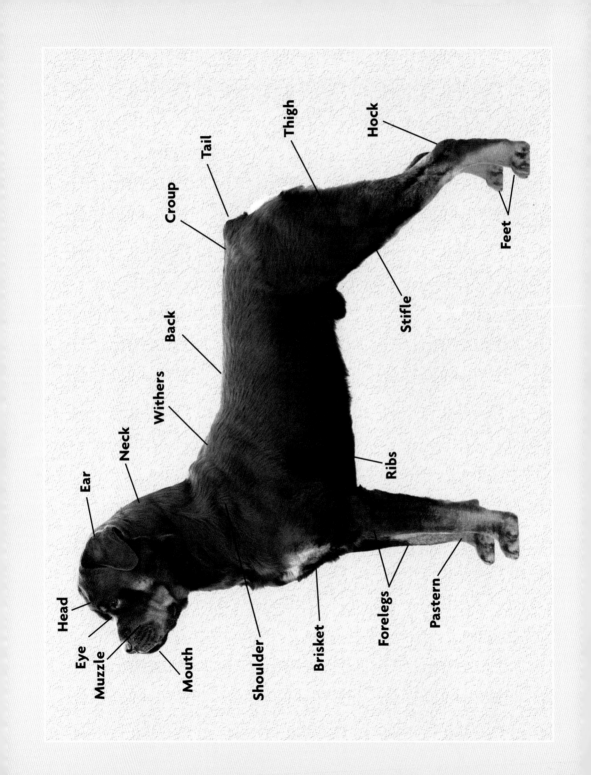

Breed Standard for the Rottweiler

Each breed of pure-bred dog has an accepted breed standard, a written description of what breeders and judges agree is the perfect dog; in this case, the perfect Rottweiler. The national breed club—the ADRK in Germany, the American Rottweiler Club in the U.S., etc.—draws up a standard and it is submitted to the national kennel club (the German Kennel Club, the American Kennel Club, etc). Once the national club accepts the standard, the breed is "recognized" and the standard becomes the guide for the fancy to evaluate the quality of each individual animal. Of course, no dog can be completely perfect according to the standard, but breeders continually try to breed closer and closer to that perfect Rottweiler.

Though breeders strive for perfection in their dogs, and some come close, there is no such thing as a "perfect" Rottweiler.

Bitches—22 inches to 25 inches, with preferred size being mid-range of each sex. Correct proportion is of primary importance, as long as size is within the standard's range.

The length of body is slightly longer than the height of the dog at the withers (ratio 9 to 10). The Rottweiler is neither coarse nor shelly. Depth of chest is approximately 50% of the height of the dog. His bone and muscle mass must be sufficient to balance his frame, giving a compact and very powerful appearance.

Head: Of medium length, broad between the ears; forehead line seen in profile is moderately arched; zygomatic arch and stop well developed with strong broad upper and lower jaws. Forehead is preferred dry, however some

> You may want to have a trusted breeder evaluate your Rottweiler's conformation before deciding to show your dog.

Following is an excerpt from the AKC breed standard for the Rottweiler.

THE AMERICAN KENNEL CLUB STANDARD FOR THE ROTTWEILER

General Appearance: The ideal Rottweiler is a medium large, robust and powerful dog, black with clearly defined rust markings. His compact and substantial build denotes great strength, agility and endurance. Dogs are characteristically more massive throughout with larger frame and heavier bone than bitches. Bitches are distinctly feminine, but without weakness of substance or structure.

> Head skin should not be loose, though a modest wrinkle when the dog is attentive is acceptable.

Size, Proportion, Substance: *Dogs*—24 inches to 27 inches.

wrinkling may occur when dog is alert. Expression is noble, alert, and self-assured. Eyes of medium size, almond shaped with well fitting lids, moderately deep-set, neither protruding nor receding. The desired color is a uniform dark brown. Ears of medium size, pendant, triangular in shape; when carried alertly the ears are level with the top of the skull and appear to broaden it. Ears are to be set well apart, hanging forward with the inner edge lying tightly against the head and terminating at approximately mid-cheek. *Muzzle*—Bridge is straight, broad at base with slight tapering towards tip. Nose is broad rather than round and always black. *Lips*—Always black; corners closed; inner mouth pigment is preferred dark.

Neck, Topline, Body: *Neck*—Powerful, well muscled, moderately long, slightly arched and without loose skin. *Topline*—The back is firm and level, extending in a straight line from behind the withers to the croup. The back remains horizontal to the ground while the dog is moving or standing. *Body*—The chest is roomy, broad and deep, reaching to elbow, with well pronounced forechest and well sprung, oval ribs. Back is straight and strong. Loin is short, deep and well muscled. Croup is broad, of medium length and only slightly

Rottweilers are required to have a scissors bite. The upper teeth should slightly overlap the lower teeth.

sloping. Underline of a mature Rottweiler has a slight tuck-up. *Tail*—Tail docked short, close to body, leaving one or two tail vertebrae. The set of the tail is more important than length. Properly set, it gives an impression of elongation of topline.

Forequarters: Shoulder blade is long and well laid back. Legs are strongly developed with straight, heavy bone, not set close together. Pasterns are strong, springy and almost perpendicular to the ground. Feet are round, compact with well arched toes, turning neither in nor out. Dewclaws may be removed.

Hindquarters: Angulation of hindquarters balances that of forequarters. Upper thigh is fairly long, very broad and well muscled. Stifle joint is well turned. Lower thigh is long, broad and powerful, with extensive muscling leading into a strong hock joint. Rear pasterns are nearly perpendicular to the ground. Feet are somewhat longer than the front feet, turning neither in nor out. Pads are thick and hard. Dewclaws must be removed.

Coat: Outer coat is straight, coarse, dense, of medium length and lying flat. Undercoat should be present on neck and thighs. Undercoat should not show through outer coat. The coat is shortest on head, ears and legs, longest on breeching. The Rottweiler is to be exhibited in the natural condition with no trimming.

Color: Always black with rust to mahogany markings. The demarcation between black and rust is to be clearly defined. The undercoat is gray, tan, or black.

Gait: The Rottweiler is a trotter. His movement should be balanced, harmonious, sure, powerful and unhindered, with strong forereach and a powerful rear drive. The motion is effortless, efficient, and ground-covering. As speed increases the legs will converge under body towards a center line.

Temperament: The Rottweiler is basically a calm, confident and courageous dog with a self-assured aloofness that does not lend itself to immediate and indiscriminate friendships. A Rottweiler is self-confident and responds quietly and with a wait-and-see attitude to influences in his environment. He has an inherent desire to protect home and family, and is an intelligent dog of extreme hardness and adaptability with a strong willingness to work, making him especially suited as a companion, guardian and general all-purpose dog.

Disqualifications: Entropion, ectropion. Overshot, undershot (when incisors do not touch or mesh); wry mouth; two or more missing teeth. Unilateral cryptorchid or cryptorchid males. Long coat. Any base color other than black; absence of all markings.

	CORRECT	**INCORRECT**

EARS
Skull should be broad between ears; ears should lie flat and close to cheek.

FOREQUARTERS
Chest should be roomy and broad; legs should be straight and should look strong and muscular.

HINDQUARTERS
Legs should be strong, with musculature apparent in both upper and lower thigh, and no exaggeration.

BACK
Should be straight and strong, and should appear stable both in motion and at rest. Should not have a roach back (1) or sway back (2).

1

2

Your Puppy
Rottweiler

ARE YOU A ROTTWEILER PERSON?

Have you ever been to the home of a friend or relative who owned a large, unruly dog? This untrained, attention-starved creature hurls himself at company, climbing up on your lap, mounting your leg, and the like. Of course, the owner does not seem to notice and has no means to discipline or control the animal. A nuisance, at least; a crime, maybe! You must make a very difficult choice here. Do you really want the responsibility of owning and training a Rottweiler? He is a demanding animal. He is

also very smart and needs your total concentration. A primary consideration is time, not only the time of the animal's allotted life-span, which can be eight to ten years or more, but also the time required for the owner to exercise and care for the creature. If you are not committed to the welfare and whole existence of this energetic, purposeful animal; if, in the simplest, most basic example, you are not willing to walk your dog daily, despite the weather, do not choose a Rottweiler as a companion.

Space is another important consideration. The Rottweiler in early puppyhood may be well accommodated in a corner of your

Owning a Rottweiler puppy is similar to raising a child. Puppies are just as demanding as children...but puppyhood is a lot shorter than childhood.

kitchen but, after only six months, when the dog is likely over 60 or 70 pounds, a larger space certainly will be required. A yard with a fence is also a basic and reasonable expectation.

In addition, there are the usual problems associated with puppies of any breed like the damages likely to be sustained by your floors, furniture and flowers, and, not least of all, restrictions to your freedom (of movement), as in vacation or weekend trips. This union is a serious affair and should be deeply considered, but once decided, your choice of a Rottweiler can be the most rewarding of all breeds. A few suggestions will help in the purchase of your dog.

PURCHASING THE ROTTWEILER PUPPY

Most likely you are seeking a pet Rottweiler, not necessarily a show dog. That does not mean that you are looking for a second-rate model. A "pet-quality" Rottweiler is not like a second-hand car or a "slightly irregular" sports coat. Your pet must be as sound, healthy and temperamentally fit as any top show dog. Pet owners do not want a Rottweiler who can't run smoothly and easily, who is not trustworthy and reliable around children and strangers, who does not look like a Rottweiler. You are not buying a black hound dog, you want a

Rottweiler—a handsome guard dog with a nice expression and head, sound hips, good eyes, correct markings and a lovable personality. If these qualities are not important to you as a Rottweiler owner, then perhaps you should consider another breed or even a mixed breed.

REGISTRATION CERTIFICATE AND PEDIGREE

Too often new owners are confused between these two important documents. Your puppy's pedigree, essentially a family tree, is a written record of a dog's genealogy of three generations or more. The pedigree will show you the names as well as performance titles of all the dogs in your pup's background. Your breeder must provide you with a registration application, with his part properly filled out. You must complete the application and send it to the AKC with the proper fee. Every puppy must come from a litter that has been AKC-registered by the breeder, born in the USA and from a sire and dam that are also registered with the AKC.

The seller must provide you with complete records to identify the puppy. The AKC requires that the seller provide the buyer with the following: breed; sex, color and markings; date of birth; litter number (when available); names and registration numbers of the parents; breeder's name; and date sold or delivered.

The safest method of obtaining your new Rottweiler puppy is to seek out a reputable breeder. This is suggested even if you are not looking for a show specimen. The novice breeders and pet owners who advertise at attractive prices in the local newspapers are probably kind enough towards their dogs, but likely do not have the expertise or facilities required to successfully raise these animals. These pet puppies are frequently badly weaned and left with their mother too long without the supplemental feeding required by this fast-growing breed. This lack of proper feeding can cause indigestion, rickets, weak bones, poor teeth and other problems. Veterinary bills may soon distort initial savings into financially, or worse, emotional loss.

Inquire about inoculations and when the puppy was last dosed for worms. Check the ears for any signs of mites or irritation. Are the eyes clear and free of any debris? The puppy coat is softer than the adult coat, but the coat should still be jet black and the tan markings should be visible, if not as pronounced as on the dam. Your puppy should have a dark nose and, preferably, dark toenails. This is a consideration of pigmentation, which should not be confused with color. It is wise to choose a puppy with deep rich pigmentation and as much black as possible. Deep brown eyes are best in the Rottie. Look for expression in your puppy's eyes, as this is a good sign of intelligence.

Note the way your choice moves. The Rottweiler, even in puppyhood, should show sound, deliberate movement with no tendency to stumble or drag the hind feet. Do not mistake a little puppy awkwardness for a physical defect. Most Rottweiler puppies are not skilled at coordinating their big paws perfectly just yet. Look at the mouth to make sure that the bite is fairly even, although maturity can often

BOY OR GIRL?

An important consideration to be discussed is the sex of your puppy. For a family companion, a bitch may be the better choice, considering the female's inbred concern for all young creatures and her accompanying tolerance and patience. It is always advisable to spay a pet bitch, which may guarantee her a longer life.

correct errors present at puppy-hood. If you have any doubts, ask to see the parents' mouths. This brings up an important point—do not purchase a puppy without first seeing at least one of the parents. Usually the dam is on location, though the sire often is not.

COMMITMENT OF OWNERSHIP
After considering all of these factors, you have most likely already made some very important decisions about selecting your puppy. You have chosen the Rottweiler, which means that you have decided which characteristics you want in a dog and what type of dog will best fit into your family and lifestyle. If you have selected a breeder, you have gone a step further—you have done your research and found a respon-

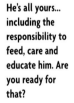

> **QUALITY FOOD**
> The cost of food must be mentioned. All dogs need a good-quality food with an adequate supply of protein to develop their bones and muscles properly. Most dogs are not picky eaters but, unless fed properly, can quickly succumb to skin problems.

sible, conscientious person who breeds quality Rottweilers and who should be a reliable source of help as you and your puppy adjust to life together. If you have observed a litter in action, you have obtained a firsthand look at the dynamics of a puppy "pack" and, thus, you have gotten to learn about each pup's individual personality—perhaps you have even found one that particularly appeals to you.

However, even if you have not yet found the Rottweiler puppy of your dreams, observing pups will help you learn to recognize certain behavior and to determine what a pup's behavior indicates about his temperament. You will be able to pick out which pups are the leaders, which ones are less outgoing, which ones are confident, which ones are shy, playful, friendly, aggressive, etc. Equally as important, you will learn to recognize what a healthy pup should look and act like. All of these things will help you in your search, and when you find the Rottweiler that

He's all yours... including the responsibility to feed, care and educate him. Are you ready for that?

ground. Buying a puppy is not—or
should not be—just another whim-
sical purchase. In fact, this is one
instance in which you actually *do*
get to choose your own family!
But, you may be thinking, buying
a puppy should be fun—it should
not be so serious and so much
work. If you keep in mind the
thought that your puppy is not a
cuddly stuffed toy or decorative
lawn ornament, but instead that
this puppy will become a real
member of your family, you will
realize that buying a puppy is not
something to be taken lightly.
Relax...the fun will start when the
pup comes home!

Always keep in mind that a
puppy is nothing more than a
baby in a furry disguise...a baby
who is virtually helpless in a
human world and who trusts his
owner for fulfillment of his basic
needs for survival. That goes
beyond food, water and shelter;
your pup needs care, protection,
guidance and love. If you are not
prepared to commit to this, then
you are not prepared to own a
dog.

"Wait a minute," you say.
"How hard could this be? All of
my neighbors own dogs and they
seem to be doing just fine. Why
should I have to worry about all of
this?" Well, you *should not* worry
about it; in fact, you will probably
find that once your Rottweiler pup
gets used to his new home, he will
fall into his place in the family

was meant for you, you will
know it!

Researching your breed, selecting a responsible breeder and
observing as many pups as possible are all important steps on the
way to dog ownership. It may
seem like a lot of effort...and you
have not even brought the pup
home yet! Remember, though, you
cannot be too careful when it
comes to deciding on the type of
dog you want and finding out
about your prospective pup's back-

quite naturally. But it never hurts to emphasize the commitment of dog ownership. With some time and patience, it is really not too difficult to raise a curious and exuberant Rottweiler pup to be a well-adjusted and well-mannered adult dog—a dog that could be your most loyal friend.

PREPARING PUPPY'S PLACE IN YOUR HOME

Researching your breed and finding a breeder are only two aspects of the "homework" you will have to do before bringing your Rottweiler puppy home. You will also have to prepare your home and family for the new addition. Much like you would prepare a nursery for a newborn baby, you will need to designate a place in your home that will be the puppy's own. How you prepare your home will depend on how much freedom the dog will be allowed: will he be confined to one room or a specific area in the house, or will he be allowed to roam as he pleases? Will he spend most of his time in the house or will he be primarily an outdoor dog? Whatever you decide, you must ensure that he has a place that he can "call his own."

When you bring your new puppy into your home, you are bringing him into what will become his home as well. Obviously, you did not buy a puppy so that he could take control of your

house, but in order for a puppy to grow into a stable, well-adjusted dog, he has to feel comfortable in his surroundings. Remember, he is leaving the warmth and security of his mother and littermates, plus the familiarity of the only place he has ever known, so it is important to make his transition as easy as possible. By preparing a place in your home for the puppy, you are making him feel as welcome as possible in a strange new place. It should not take him long to get used to it, but the sudden shock of being transplanted is somewhat traumatic for a young pup. Imagine how a small child would feel in the same situation—that is how your puppy must be feeling. It is up to you to reassure him and to let him know, "Little fellow, you are going to like it here!"

Children and Rottweilers get along very well together once *both* understand the rules of the household.

WHAT YOU SHOULD BUY

CRATE

To someone unfamiliar with the use of crates in dog training, it may seem like punishment to shut a dog in a crate; this is not the case at all. Crates are not cruel—crates have many humane and highly effective uses in dog care and training. For example, crate training is a very popular and very successful housebreaking method; a crate can keep your dog safe during travel; and, perhaps most importantly, a crate provides your dog with a place of his own in your home. It serves as a "doggie bedroom" of sorts—your Rottweiler can curl up in his crate when he wants to sleep or when he just needs a break. Many dogs sleep in their crates overnight. When lined with soft blankets and with a favorite toy, a crate becomes a cozy pseudo-den for your dog. Like his ancestors, he too will seek out the comfort and retreat of a den—you just happen to be providing him with something a little more luxurious than leaves and twigs lining a dirty ditch.

As far as purchasing a crate, the type that you buy is up to you. It will most likely be one of the two most popular types: wire or fiberglass. There are advantages and disadvantages to each type. For example, a wire crate is more open, allowing the air to flow through and affording the dog a view of what is going on around him. A fiberglass crate, however, is sturdier and can double as a travel crate since it provides more protection for the dog. The size of the crate is another thing to consider. Puppies do not stay

Your local pet shop will have the crate best suited for your Rottweiler. Get the largest size suitable; while a small crate is satisfactory for your puppy, it won't be large enough when the dog matures.

puppies forever—in fact, sometimes it seems as if they grow right before your eyes. A small crate may be fine for a very young Rottweiler pup, but it will not do him much good for long! Unless you have the money and the inclination to buy a new crate every time your pup has a growth spurt, it is better to get one that will accommodate your dog both as a pup and at full size. A giant crate will be necessary for a full-grown Rottweiler, as the approximate weight range is between 75 and 110 pounds and he stands as tall as 27 inches at the shoulder.

BEDDING

A soft crate pad and a blanket in the dog's crate will help the dog feel more at home. First, the bedding will take the place of the leaves, twigs, etc., that the pup would use in the wild to make a den; the pup can make his own "burrow" in the crate. Although your pup is far removed from his den-making ancestors, the denning

your dog will enjoy playing with his favorite toys, while you will enjoy the fact that they distract him from your expensive shoes and leather sofa. Puppies love to chew; in fact, chewing is a physical need for pups as they are teething, and everything looks appetizing! The full range of your possessions—from cotton slipper to Oriental rug—is fair game in the eyes of a teething pup. Puppies are not all that discerning when it comes to finding something to literally "sink their teeth into"— everything tastes great!

Stuffed toys are another option; these are good to put in

Be prepared for your pup's arrival. Ask your breeder to recommend the equipment you will need.

instinct is still a part of his genetic makeup. Second, until you bring your pup home, he has been sleeping amid the warmth of his mother and littermates, and while a blanket is not the same as a warm, breathing body, it still provides heat and something with which to snuggle. You will want to wash your pup's bedding frequently in case he has an accident in his crate, and replace or remove any blanket or padding that becomes ragged and starts to fall apart.

Toys

Toys are a must for dogs of all ages, especially for curious playful pups. Puppies are the "children" of the dog world, and what child does not love toys? Strong, durable chew toys provide enjoyment to both dog and owner—

CRATE-TRAINING TIPS

During crate training, you should partition off the section of the crate in which the pup stays. If he is given too big an area, this will hinder your training efforts. Crate training is based on the fact that a dog does not like to soil his sleeping quarters, so it is ineffective to keep a pup in an area that is so big that he can eliminate in one end and get far enough away from it to sleep. Also, you want to make the crate den-like for the pup. Blankets and a favorite toy will make the crate cozy for the small pup; as he grows, you may want to evict some of his "roommates" to make more room. It will take some coaxing at first, but be patient. Given some time to get used to it, your pup will adapt to his new home-within-a-home quite nicely.

the pup's crate to give him some company. Be careful of these, as a pup can de-stuff one pretty quickly, and stay away from stuffed toys with small plastic eyes or parts that a pup could choke on. Similarly, squeaky toys are quite popular. There are dogs that will come running from

anywhere in the house at the first sound from their favorite squeaky friend. Again, if a pup de-stuffs one of these, the small plastic squeaker inside can be dangerous if swallowed. Monitor the condition of your pup's toys carefully and get rid of any that have been chewed to the point of becoming potentially harmful.

Be careful of natural bones, which have a tendency to splinter into sharp, dangerous pieces. Also be careful of rawhide, which after enough chewing can turn into pieces that are easy to swallow, and also watch out for the mushy mess it can turn into on your carpet.

TOYS, TOYS, TOYS!

With a big variety of dog toys available, and so many that look like they would be a lot of fun for a dog, be careful in your selection. It is amazing what a set of puppy teeth can do to a toy; so, obviously, safety is a major consideration. Be sure to choose the most durable products that you can find for the strong-jawed Rottie. Hard nylon bones and toys are a safe bet, and many of them are offered in different scents and flavors that will be sure to capture your dog's attention. It is always fun to play a game of fetch with your dog, and there are balls and flying discs that are specially made to withstand dog teeth.

LEASH

A nylon leash is probably the best option as it is the most resistant to puppy teeth, should your pup take a liking to chewing on his leash. Of course, this is a habit that should be nipped in the bud, but if your pup likes to chew on his leash he has a very slim chance of being able to chew through the strong nylon. Nylon leashes are also lightweight, which is good for a young Rottweiler who is just getting used to the idea of walking on a leash. For everyday walking and safety purposes, the nylon leash is a good choice. Of course there are special leashes for training purposes, and specially made leather harnesses for the working Rottweiler, but these are not neces-

sary for routine walks. If your Rottweiler is especially strong or tends to pull on the leash, you may want to purchase something stronger, like a thicker leather leash.

COLLAR

Your pup should get used to wearing a collar all the time since you will want to attach his ID tags to his collar. Also, the leash and collar go hand in hand—you have to attach the leash to something! A lightweight nylon collar will be a good choice; make sure that it fits snugly enough so that the pup cannot wriggle out of it, but loose enough so that it will not be uncomfortably tight around the pup's neck. You should be able to fit a finger in between the pup and the collar. It may take some time for your pup to get used to wearing the collar, but soon he will not even notice that it is there. Choke collars are made for training, but should only be used by an owner who knows exactly how to use it. If you use a stronger leather leash or a chain leash to walk your Rottweiler, you will need a stronger collar as well.

FOOD AND WATER BOWLS

Your pup will need two bowls, one for food and one for water. You may want two sets of bowls, one for inside and one for outside, depending on where the dog will

PET INSURANCE
Just like you can insure your car, your house and your own health, you likewise can insure your dog's health. Investigate a pet insurance policy by talking to your vet. Depending on the age of your dog, the breed and the kind of coverage you desire, your policy can be very affordable. Most policies cover accidental injuries, poisoning and thousands of medical problems and illnesses, including cancers. Some carriers also offer routine care and immunization coverage.

be fed and where he will be spending most of his time. Stainless steel or sturdy plastic bowls are popular choices. Although plastic bowls are more chewable, dogs tend not to chew on the steel variety, which can also be sterilized. Rottweiler owners should put their dogs' food and water bowls on specially made elevated stands; this brings the food closer to the dog's level so he does not have to bend down as far, thus aiding his digestion and helping to guard against bloat or gastric torsion in deep-chested dogs. It is very important to buy sturdy bowls since, again, anything is in danger of being chewed by puppy teeth and you do not want your dog to be constantly chewing apart his bowl (for his safety and for your wallet!).

He's lonesome! Your Rottweiler pup needs loving care to help him adjust to his new home.

CLEANING SUPPLIES

Untill your pup is house-trained, you will be doing a lot of cleaning. "Accidents" will occur, which is okay for now because he does not know any better. All you can do is clean up any accidents—old rags, paper towels, newspapers and a safe disinfectant are good to have on hand.

BEYOND THE BASICS

The items previously discussed are the bare necessities. You will find out what else you need as you go along—grooming supplies, flea/tick protection, baby gates to partition a room, etc.—these things will vary depending on your situation. It is just important that you have everything you need to feed and make your Rottweiler comfortable in his first few days at home.

Pet shops sell large varieties of leashes in different lengths, strengths, colors and materials. Get a top-quality leash, as it will be useful for the entire life of the dog.

PUPPY-PROOFING YOUR HOME

Aside from making sure that your Rottweiler will be comfortable in his new home, you also have to make sure that the home is safe for your Rottweiler. This means taking precautions to make sure that your pup will not get into anything he should not get into and that there is nothing within his reach that may harm him should he sniff it, chew it, inspect it, etc. This probably seems obvious since, while you are primarily concerned with your pup's safety, at the same time you do not want your belongings to be destroyed. Breakables should be placed out of reach if your dog is to have full run of the house. If he is to be limited to certain places within the house, keep any potentially dangerous items in the "off-limits" areas. An electrical cord can pose a danger should the puppy decide to taste it—and who is going to convince a pup that it would not make a great chew toy? Cords should be kept from puppy's teeth and fastened tightly

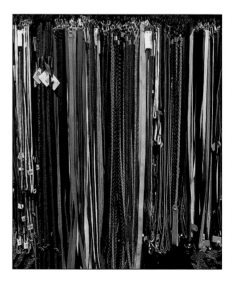

against the wall. If your dog is going to spend time in a crate, make sure that there is nothing near his crate that he can reach if he sticks his curious little nose or paws through the openings. And just as you would with a child, keep all household cleaners and chemicals where the pup cannot get to them.

It is just as important to make sure that the outside of your home is safe. Of course your puppy should never be unsupervised, but a pup let loose in the yard will want to run and explore, and he should be granted that freedom. Do not let a fence give you a false sense of security; you would be surprised how crafty (and persistent) a dog can be in figuring out how to dig under and squeeze his way through small holes, or to jump or climb over a fence. The remedy is to make the fence high enough so that it really is impossible for your dog to get over it (about 6 feet should suffice), and well embedded into the ground. Be sure to repair or secure any gaps in the fence. Check the fence periodically to ensure that it is in good shape and make repairs as needed; a very determined pup may return to the same spot to "work on it" until he is able to get through.

FIRST TRIP TO THE VET
You have picked out your puppy, your home and family are ready, now all you have to do is pick

Food and water bowls are essential for the proper care of your Rottweiler.

your Rottweiler up from the breeder and the fun begins, right? Well...not so fast. Something else you need to prepare for is your pup's first trip to the veterinarian. Perhaps the breeder can recommend someone in the area who specializes in Rottweilers or large-breed dogs, or maybe you know some other Rottweiler owners who can suggest a good vet. Either way, you should have an appointment arranged for your pup before you pick him up; plan on taking him for a checkup within the first few days of bringing him home.

The pup's first visit will consist of an overall examination to make sure that the pup does not have any problems that are not apparent to you. The veterinarian will also set up a schedule for the pup's vaccinations; the breeder will inform you of which ones the pup has already received and the vet can continue from there.

INTRODUCTION TO THE FAMILY
Everyone in the house will be excited about the puppy's coming home and will want to pet him

The yard or kennel run in which your Rottweiler is kept should be securely fenced in.

and play with him, but it is best to make the introduction low-key so as not to overwhelm the puppy. He is apprehensive already; it is the first time he has been separated from his mother and the breeder, and the ride to your home is likely the first time he has been in a car. The last thing you want to do is smother him, as this will only frighten him further. This is not to say that human contact is not extremely necessary at this stage, because this is the time when an instant connection between the pup and his human family is formed. Gentle petting and soothing words should help console him, as well as just putting him down and letting him explore on his own (under your watchful eye, of course).

The pup may approach the family members or may busy himself with exploring for a while. Gradually, each person should spend some time with the pup, one at a time, crouching down to get as close to the pup's

level as possible and letting him sniff their hands and petting him gently. He definitely needs human attention and he needs to be touched—this is how to form an immediate bond. Just remember that the pup is experiencing a lot of things for the first time, all at the same time. There are new people, new noises, new smells and new things to investigate, so be gentle, be affectionate and be as comforting as you can be.

YOUR PUP'S FIRST NIGHT AT HOME
You have traveled home with your new charge safely in his crate or on a family member's lap. He has been to the vet for a thorough checkup; he has been weighed, his papers examined; perhaps he has even been vaccinated and wormed as well. He has met the family and licked the whole family, including

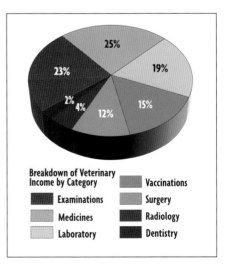

Breakdown of Veterinary Income by Category

Vaccinations	
Examinations	
Surgery	
Medicines	
Radiology	
Laboratory	
Dentistry	

25%
19%
23%
2% 4%
12%
15%

the excited children and the less-than-happy cat. He has explored his area, his new bed, the yard and anywhere else he has been permitted. He has eaten his first meal at home and relieved himself in the proper place. He has heard lots of new sounds, smelled new friends and seen more of the outside world than ever before.

That was the just the first day! He is exhausted and is ready for bed...or so you think!

It is puppy's first night and you are ready to say "Good night"—keep in mind that this is puppy's first night ever to be sleeping alone. His dam and litter-mates are no longer at paw's length and he is a bit scared, cold and lonely. Be reassuring to your new family member, but this is not the time to spoil him and give in to his inevitable whining.

Puppies whine. They whine to let the others know where they are and hopefully to get company out of it. Place your pup in his new bed or crate in his room and close the door. Mercifully, he will fall asleep without a peep. When the inevitable occurs, ignore the whin-ing; he is fine. Be strong and keep his interest in mind. Do not allow your heart to become guilty and visit the pup. He will fall asleep.

Many breeders recommend placing a piece of bedding from his former home in his new bed so that he recognizes the scent of his littermates. Others still advise placing a hot water bottle in his bed for warmth. This latter may be a good idea provided the pup does not attempt to suckle—he will get good and wet and may not fall asleep so fast.

Puppy's first night can be somewhat stressful for the pup and his new family. Remember that you are setting the tone of nighttime at your house. Unless you want to play with your pup every evening at 10 p.m., midnight and 2 a.m., do not initiate the habit. Surely your family will thank you, and so will your pup!

PREVENTING PUPPY PROBLEMS

SOCIALIZATION

Now that you have done all of the preparatory work and have helped your pup get accustomed to his new home and family, it is about time for you to have some fun! Socializing your Rottweiler pup gives you the opportunity to show off your new friend, and your pup gets to reap the benefits of being

A toy may help keep your puppy occupied and less prone to whining, nipping or other undesirable behavior.

Provide your Rottweiler with comfortable bedding. A dog in the wild would use leaves as a burrow, but a pet dog needs a proper dog bed or a blanket in a crate.

an adorable furry creature that people will adore, want to pet and, in general, think is absolutely precious!

Besides getting to know his new family, your puppy should be exposed to other people, animals and situations. This will help him become well adjusted as he grows up and less prone to being timid or fearful of the new things he will encounter. Your pup's socialization began at the breeder's; now it is your responsibility to continue. The socialization he receives up until the age of 12 weeks is the most critical, as this is the time when he forms his impressions of the outside world. Lack of socialization can manifest itself in fear and aggression as the dog grows up. He needs lots of human contact, affection, handling and exposure to other animals. Be careful during the eight-to-ten-week-old period, also known as the fear period. The interaction he receives during this time should be gentle and reassuring.

Once your pup has received his necessary vaccinations, feel free to take him out and about (on his leash, of course). Take him around the neighborhood, take him on your daily errands, let people pet him, let him meet other dogs and pets, etc. Puppies do not have to try to make friends; there will be no shortage of people who will want to introduce themselves. Just make sure that you carefully supervise each meeting. If the neighborhood children want to say hello, for example, that is great—children and pups most often make great companions. But sometimes an excited child can unintentionally handle a pup too roughly or an overzealous pup can playfully nip a little too hard. You want to make socialization experiences positive ones; what a pup learns during this very formative stage will impact his attitude toward future encounters. A pup that has a bad

PUPPY PROBLEMS

The majority of problems that are commonly seen in young pups will disappear as your dog gets older. However, how you deal with problems when he is young will determine how he reacts to discipline as an adult dog. It is important to establish who is boss (hopefully it will be you!) right away when you are first bonding with your dog. This bond will set the tone for the rest of your life together.

experience with a child may grow up to be a dog that is shy around or aggressive toward children, and you want your dog to be comfortable around everyone.

CONSISTENCY IN TRAINING

Dogs, being pack animals, naturally need a leader, or else they try to establish dominance in their packs. When you bring a dog into your family, who becomes the leader and who becomes the "pack" are entirely up to you! Your pup's intuitive quest for dominance, coupled with the fact that it is nearly impossible to look at an adorable Rottweiler pup, with his "puppy-dog" face, and not cave in, give the pup almost an unfair advantage in getting the upper hand! And a pup will definitely test the waters to see what he can and cannot get away with. Do not give in to those pleading eyes—stand your ground when it comes to disciplining the pup and make sure that all family members do the same. It will only confuse the pup when Mother tells him to get off the couch when he is used to sitting up there with Father to watch the nightly news. Avoid discrepancies by having all members of the household decide on the rules before the pup even comes home...and be consistent in enforcing them! Early training shapes the dog's personality, so you cannot be unclear in what you expect.

COMMON PUPPY PROBLEMS

The best way to prevent problems is to be proactive in stopping an undesirable behavior as soon as it starts. The old saying "You can't teach an old dog new tricks" does not necessarily hold true, but it *is* true that it is much easier to discourage bad behavior in a young developing pup than to wait until the pup's bad behavior becomes the adult dog's bad habit. There are some problems that are especially prevalent in puppies as they develop.

> ### PUP MEETS WORLD
> Thorough socialization includes not only meeting new people but also being introduced to new experiences such as riding in the car, having his coat brushed, hearing the television, walking in a crowd—the list is endless. The more your pup experiences, and the more positive the experiences are, the less of a shock and the less frightening it will be for your pup to encounter new things.

NIPPING

As puppies start to teethe, they feel the need to sink their teeth into anything...unfortunately, that includes your fingers, arms, hair, toes...whatever happens to be available. You may find this behavior cute for about the first five seconds...until you feel just how sharp those puppy teeth are. This is something you want to discourage immediately and consistently with a firm "No!" (or whatever number of firm "Nos" it takes for him to understand that you mean business) and replace your finger with an appropriate chew toy. While this behavior is merely annoying when the dog is still young, it can become danger-ous as your Rottweiler's adult teeth grow in and his jaws develop, if he thinks that it is okay to gnaw on human appendages. You do not want to take a chance with a Rottweiler; this is a breed whose jaws become naturally very strong. He does not mean any harm with a friendly nip, but he also does not know his own strength.

CRYING/WHINING

Your pup will often cry, whine, whimper, howl or make some type of commotion when he is left alone. This is basically his way of calling out for attention, to make sure that you know he is there and that you have not forgotten about him. He feels insecure when he is

left alone, for example, when you are out of the house and he is in his crate or when you are in another part of the house and he cannot see you. The noise he is making is an expression of the anxiety he feels at being alone, so he needs to be taught that being alone is okay. You are not actually

---

CHEWING TIPS

Chewing goes hand in hand with nipping in the sense that a teething puppy is always looking for a way to soothe his aching gums. In this case, instead of chewing on you, he may have taken a liking to your favorite shoe or something else which he should not be chewing. Again, realize that this is a normal canine behavior that does not need to be discouraged, only redirected. Your pup just needs to be taught what is acceptable to chew on and what is off-limits. Consis-tently tell him "No!" when you catch him chewing on something forbidden and give him a chew toy.

Conversely, praise him when you catch him chewing on something appropriate. In this way, you are discouraging the inappropriate behav-ior and reinforcing the desired behav-ior. The puppy's chewing should stop after his adult teeth have come in, but an adult dog continues to chew for various reasons—perhaps because he is bored, needs to relieve tension or just likes to chew. That is why it is important to redirect his chewing when he is still young.

training the dog to stop making noise, you are training him to feel comfortable when he is alone and thus removing the need for him to make the noise. This is where the crate with a cozy crate pad and a toy comes in handy. You want to know that he is safe when you are not there to supervise, and you know that he will be safe in his crate rather than roaming freely about the house. In order for the pup to stay in his crate without making a fuss, he needs to be comfortable in his crate. On that note, it is extremely important that the crate is never used as a form of punishment, or the pup will develop a negative association with the crate.

Accustom the pup to the crate in short, gradually increasing time intervals in which you put him in the crate, maybe with a treat, and stay in the room with him. If he cries or makes a fuss, do not go to him, but stay in his sight. Gradually he will realize that staying in his crate is okay without your help, and it will not be so trau-

A puppy looks to and trusts his owner for care and guidance.

matic for him when you are not around. You may want to leave the radio on softly when you leave the house; the sound of human voices may be comforting to him.

MANNERS MATTER

During the socialization process, a puppy should meet people, experience different environments and definitely be exposed to other canines. Through playing and interacting with other dogs, your puppy will learn lessons, ranging from controlling the pressure of his jaws by biting his littermates to the inner-workings of the canine pack that he will apply to his human relationships for the rest of his life. That is why removing a puppy from the litter too early (before eight weeks) can be detrimental to the pup's development.

INTERNAL ORGANS OF THE ROTTWEILER

1. Esophagus
2. Lungs
3. Gall Bladder
4. Liver
5. Kidney
6. Stomach
7. Intestines
8. Urinary Bladder

Everyday Care of Your Rottweiler

DIETARY AND FEEDING CONSIDERATIONS

In today's world, the Rottweiler owner has hundreds of choices for feeding his dog. The pet shop offers dozens of brands in dozens of varieties: from the puppy diet to the lamb and rice to the senior diet to the hypoallergenic to the low-calorie! Since your Rottweiler's nutrition is related to his coat, health and temperament, you want to offer him the best possible diet, fit for a Rottweiler of his age. Dedicated owners, however, can become perplexed by the vast number of choices. Even those people who truly want to feed their dogs the best often cannot do so because they do not know which foods are best for their particular dogs.

Dog foods are produced in three basic types: dry, semi-moist

Follow the advice of the breeder from whom you bought your Rottweiler when it comes to food.

and canned. Dry foods are for the cost-conscious because they are much less expensive than semi-moist and canned. Dry foods contain the least fat and the most preservatives. Most canned foods are 60–70% water, while semi-moist foods are so full of sugar that they are the least preferred by owners, though dogs welcome them (as does a child sweets).

Three stages of development must be considered when selecting a diet for your dog: the puppy stage, the adult stage and the senior stage.

Puppy Stage

Puppies have a natural instinct to suck milk from their mother's teats. They should exhibit this behavior the first day of their lives. If they don't suckle within a few hours, the breeder attempts to

---

STORING DOG FOOD

You must store your dry dog food carefully. Open packages of dog food quickly lose their vitamin value, usually within 90 days of being opened. Mold spores and vermin could also contaminate the food.

put them onto their mother's nipples. Their failure to feed means the breeder has to feed them himself, perhaps with the guidance of a vet. This will involve a baby bottle and a special formula. Their mother's milk is much better than any formula because it contains colostrum, a sort of antibiotic milk that protects the puppies during the first eight to ten weeks of their lives.

Puppies should be allowed to nurse for six weeks and they should be slowly weaned away from their mother by introducing small portions of canned meat after they are about one month old.

By the time they are eight weeks old, they should be completely weaned and fed solely a puppy food. During this weaning period, their diet is most important as the puppies grow fastest during the first year of life.

> **FEEDING TIPS**
> • Dog food must be served at room temperature, neither too hot nor too cold. Fresh water, changed often and served in a clean bowl, is mandatory, especially when feeding dry food.
> • Never feed your dog from the table while you are eating, and never feed your dog leftovers from your own meal. They usually contain too much fat and too much seasoning.
> • Dogs must chew their food. Hard pellets are excellent; soups and stews are to be avoided.
> • Don't add leftovers or any extras to commercial dog food. The normal food is usually balanced, and adding something extra destroys the balance.
> • Except for age-related changes, dogs do not require dietary variations. They can be fed the same diet, day after day, without becoming bored or ill.

A shiny coat and alert demeanor are two signs that your Rottweiler is getting the proper nutrition.

Growth foods can be recommended by your vet, and your puppy should be kept on this diet for up to 18 months. Puppy diets should be balanced for your dog's needs and supplements of vitamins, minerals and protein should not be necessary.

ADULT DIETS

A dog is considered an adult when he has stopped growing. The growth is in height and/or length. Do not consider the dog's weight when the decision is made to switch from a puppy diet to a maintenance diet. A Rottweiler reaches adulthood at about two years of age, though some dogs fully mature at 16 months, while others may take up to three years. Again you should rely upon your vet to recommend an acceptable maintenance diet. Major dog food manufacturers specialize in this type of food and it is just necessary for you to select the one best suited to your dog's needs. Active dogs may have different requirements than sedate dogs.

SENIOR DIETS

As a dog gets older, his metabolism changes. The older dog usually exercises less, moves more slowly and sleeps more. This change in lifestyle and physiological performance requires a change in diet. Since these changes take place slowly, they might not be recognizable. What is easily recognizable is weight gain. By continuing to feed your dog an adult maintenance diet when he is slowing down metabolically, your dog will gain weight. Obesity in an older dog compounds the health problems that already accompany old age.

As your dog gets older, few of his organs function up to par. The kidneys slow down and the intestines become less efficient. These age-related factors are best handled with a change in diet

and a change in feeding schedule to give smaller portions that are more easily digested.

There is no single best diet for every older dog. While many dogs do well on light or senior diets, other dogs do better on puppy diets or other special premium diets such as lamb and rice.

Be sensitive to your senior Rottweiler's diet and this will help control other problems that may arise with your old friend.

GRAIN-BASED DIETS

Some less expensive dog foods are based on grains and other plant proteins. While these products may appear to be attractively priced, many breeders prefer a diet based on animal proteins and believe that they are more conducive to your dog's health. Many grain-based diets rely on soy protein, which may cause flatulence (passing gas).

There are many cases, however, when your dog might require a special diet. These special requirements should only be recommended by your veterinarian.

Walking your Rottweiler daily is the very least amount of exercise your dog will require. You can be certain that you will be well guarded during your walk.

While not as hyper as a hunting dog, the Rottweiler is still an active working dog that can be trained to excel in various pursuits. This Rottie is practicing for an agility trial.

WATER

Just as your dog needs proper nutrition from his food, water is an essential "nutrient"' as well. Water keeps the dog's body properly hydrated and promotes normal function of the body's systems. During housebreaking, it is necessary to keep an eye on how much water your Rottweiler is drinking, but once he is reliably trained he should have access to clean fresh water at all times. Make sure that the dog's water bowl is clean, and change the water often. As some vets have recommended, do not leave water bowls down when feeding your dog. This practice can help to prevent the onset of bloat in the Rottweiler.

EXERCISE

Exercising a Rottweiler is not as time-consuming as it may seem. The Rottweiler is a working dog, not a field dog that has pent-up energy or a racing dog that has long legs to stretch. All dogs require some form of exercise, regardless of breed. A sedentary lifestyle is as harmful to a dog as it is to a person. The Rottweiler happens to be a fairly active breed that requires more exercise than, say, an English Bulldog, but you don't have to be a weightlifter or marathon runner to provide your dog with the exercise he needs. Regular walks, play sessions in the yard and letting the dog run free

in the fenced yard under your supervision are all sufficient forms of exercise for the Rottweiler. For those who are more ambitious, you will find that your adult Rottweiler will be able to keep up with you on extra-long walks or the morning run. Do not expose your Rottie pup to strenuous or vigorous exercise until he is at least 12 months of age. Such activity can harm his growing bones and ligaments. Not only is exercise essential to keep the dog's body fit, it is essential to his mental well-being. A bored dog will find something to do, which often manifests itself in some type of destructive behavior. In this sense, it is essential for your mental well-being as well!

A once-over with a hound glove like this one will give your Rottweiler's black coat polish and shine.

GROOMING

BRUSHING

A natural bristle brush, a slicker brush or even a hound glove can be used for regular routine brushing. Grooming is effective for removing dead hair and stimulating the dog's natural oils to add shine and a healthy look to the coat. Your Rottweiler is not a breed that needs excessive grooming, but his coat needs to be brushed every few days as part of routine maintenance. Regular brushing will get rid of dust and dandruff and remove any dead hair. Regular grooming sessions are also a good way to spend time with your dog. Many dogs grow to like the feel of being brushed and will enjoy the regular routine.

BATHING

Dogs do not need to be bathed as often as humans, but occasional bathing is essential for healthy skin and a healthy, shiny coat. Again, like most anything, if you accustom your pup to being bathed as a puppy, it will be second nature by the time he grows up. You want your dog to be at ease in the bath or else it could end up a wet, soapy, messy ordeal for both of you!

Brush your Rottweiler thoroughly before wetting his coat. This will get rid of most of the dead coat. Make sure that your dog has a good non-slip surface to stand on. Begin by wetting the dog's coat. A shower or hose attachment is necessary for thoroughly wetting and rinsing the coat. Check the water temperature to make sure that it is neither too hot nor too cold for the dog.

Next, apply shampoo to the dog's coat and work it into a good lather. You should purchase a shampoo that is made for dogs; do not use a product made for human hair. Wash the head last; you do not want shampoo to drip into the dog's eyes while you are washing the rest of his body. Work the shampoo all the way down to the skin. You can use this opportunity to check the skin for any bumps, bites or other abnormalities. Do not neglect any area of the body—get all of the hard-to-reach places.

Once the dog has been thoroughly shampooed, he requires an equally thorough rinsing. Shampoo left in the coat can become irritating to the skin. Protect his

---

SOAP IT UP

The use of human soap products like shampoo, bubble bath and hand soap can be damaging to a dog's coat and skin. Human products are too strong; they remove the protective oils coating the dog's hair and skin that make him water-resistant. Use only shampoo made especially for dogs. You may like to use a medicated shampoo, which will help to keep external parasites at bay.

eyes from the shampoo by shielding them with your hand and directing the flow of water in the opposite direction. You should also avoid getting water in the ear canal. Be prepared for your dog to shake out his coat—you might want to stand back, but make sure you have a hold on the dog to keep him from running through the house.

EAR CLEANING

The ears should be kept clean and any excess hair inside the ear should be trimmed. Ears can be cleaned with a cotton ball and special cleaner or ear powder made especially for dogs. Be on the lookout for any signs of infection or ear-mite infestation. If your Rottweiler is shaking his head or scratching at his ears frequently, this usually indicates a problem. If his ears have an unusual odor, this is a sure sign of mite infestation or infection, and a signal to have his ears checked by the vet.

NAIL CLIPPING

Your Rottweiler should be accustomed to having his nails trimmed at an early age, since it will be part of your maintenance routine throughout his life. Not only does it look nicer, but a dog with long nails can cause injury if he jumps up or if he scratches someone unintentionally. Also, a long nail has a better chance of ripping and bleeding, or of causing the feet to spread. A good rule of thumb is

BATHING BEAUTY

Once you are sure that the dog is thoroughly rinsed, squeeze the excess water out of his coat with your hand and dry him with a heavy towel. You may choose to use a blow dryer (on "low") on his coat or just let it dry naturally. In cold weather, never allow your dog outside with a wet coat.

There are "dry bath" products on the market, which are sprays and powders intended for spot cleaning that can be used between regular baths if necessary. They are not substitutes for regular baths, but they are easy to use for touch-ups as they do not require rinsing.

that if you can hear your dog's nails clicking on the floor when he walks, his nails are too long.

Before you start cutting, make sure you can identify the "quick" in each nail. The quick is a blood vessel that runs through the center of each nail and grows rather close to the end. It will bleed if acciden-

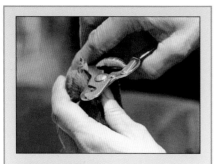

PEDICURE TIP

A dog that spends a lot of time outside on a hard surface, such as cement or pavement, will have his nails naturally worn down and may not need to have them trimmed as often, except maybe in the colder months when he is not outside as much. Regardless, it is best to get your dog accustomed to the nail-trimming procedure at an early age so that he is used to it. Some dogs are especially sensitive about having their feet touched, but if a dog has experienced it since puppyhood, it should not bother him.

at a time, particularly with black-nailed dogs.

Hold your pup steady as you begin trimming his nails; you do not want him to make any sudden movements or run away. Talk to him soothingly and stroke him as you clip. Holding his foot in your hand, simply take off the end of each nail in one quick clip. You can purchase nail clippers that are specially made for dogs; you can probably find them wherever you buy pet supplies.

TRAVELING WITH YOUR DOG

CAR TRAVEL

You should accustom your Rottweiler to riding in a car at an early age. You may or may not often take him in the car, but at the very least he will need to go to the vet and you do not want these trips to be traumatic for the dog or a big hassle for you. The safest way for a dog to ride in the car is in his crate.

The safest method of traveling with a Rottie is in his own crate or specially designed compartment.

tally cut, which will be quite painful for the dog as it contains nerve endings. Keep some type of clotting agent on hand, such as a styptic pencil or styptic powder (the type used for shaving). This will stop the bleeding quickly when applied to the end of the cut nail. Do not panic if this happens, just stop the bleeding and talk soothingly to your dog. Once he has calmed down, move on to the next nail. It is better to clip a little

If he uses a fiberglass crate in the house, you can use the same crate for travel. If you have a wire crate in the house, consider purchasing an appropriately sized fiberglass or wooden crate for traveling. Wire crates can be used for travel, but fiberglass or wooden crates are safer.

Put the pup in the crate and see how he reacts. If he seems uneasy, you can have a passenger hold him on his lap while you drive. Another option is a specially made safety harness for dogs, which straps the dog in much like a seat belt. Do not let the dog roam loose in the vehicle—this is *very* dangerous! If you should stop short, your dog can be thrown and injured. If the dog starts climbing on you and pestering you while you are driving, you will not be able to concentrate on the road. It is an unsafe situation for everyone—human and canine.

For long trips, be prepared to stop to let the dog relieve himself. Bring along whatever you need to clean up after him. You should bring along some towels and paper towels, should he have an accident in the car or become carsick.

AIR TRAVEL

Contact your chosen airline before proceeding with your travel plans that include your Rottweiler. The dog will be required to travel in a fiberglass crate and you should always check in advance with the

---

COLLAR REQUIRED

If your dog gets lost, he is not able to ask for directions home. Identification tags fastened to the collar give important information—the dog's name, the owner's name, the owner's address and a telephone number where the owner can be reached. This makes it easy for whomever finds the dog to contact the owner and arrange to have the dog returned. An added advantage is that a person will be more likely to approach a lost dog who has ID tags on his collar; it tells the person that this is somebody's pet rather than a stray. This is the easiest and fastest method of identification, provided that the tags stay on the collar and the collar stays on the dog.

---

airline regarding specific requirements for the crate's size, type and labeling. To help put the dog at ease, give him one of his favorite toys in the crate. Do not feed the dog for several hours prior to checking in so that you minimize his need to relieve himself. Some airlines require that the dog must be fed within a certain time frame of arriving at the airport; in any case, before traveling a light meal is best.

Make sure your dog is properly identified and that your contact information appears on his ID tags and on his crate. Since dogs travel in a different area of the airplane than the human passengers, it is critical to follow all of the airline's instructions to the letter, so as not to become separated from your Rottweiler. There is nothing more frightening than arriving at Boston airport to learn that your Rottie missed his connecting flight in Newark!

VACATIONS AND BOARDING

So you want to take a family vacation—and you want to include *all* members of the family. You would probably make arrangements for accommodations ahead of time anyway, but this is especially important when traveling with a dog. You do not want to make an overnight stop at the only place around for miles to find out that they do not allow dogs. Also, you do not want to reserve a place for your family without mentioning that you are bringing a dog, because if it is against their policy you may not have a place to stay.

Alternatively, if you are traveling and choose not to bring your Rottweiler, you will have to make arrangements for him while you are away. Some options are to bring him to a neighbor's house to stay while you are gone, to have a familiar neighbor stop by often or stay at your house or to bring your dog to a reputable boarding kennel. If you choose to board him at a kennel, you should stop by to see the facility and where the dogs are kept to make sure that it is clean and suitably spacious. Talk to some of the employees and see how they treat the dogs—do they spend time with the dogs, play with them, exercise them, etc.? You know that your Rottweiler will not be happy unless he gets regular activity. Also find out the kennel's policy on vaccinations and what they require. This is for all of the dogs' safety, since when dogs are kept together, there is a greater risk of diseases being passed from dog to dog. Most facilities require owners to provide proof of vaccination.

IDENTIFICATION

Your Rottweiler is your valued companion and friend. That is why you always keep a close eye on him and you have made sure that he cannot escape from the garden or wriggle out of his collar and run away from you. However, accidents can happen and there may come a time when your dog unexpectedly gets separated from you. If this unfortunate event should occur, the first thing on your mind will be finding him. Proper identification will increase the chances of his being returned.

TRAVEL TIP
Never leave your dog alone in the car. In hot weather, your dog can die from the high temperature inside a closed vehicle; even a car parked in the shade can heat up very quickly. Leaving the window open is dangerous as well since the dog can hurt himself trying to get out.

Training Your Rottweiler

Living with an untrained dog is a lot like owning a piano that you do not know how to play—it is a nice object to look at, but it does not do much more than that to bring you pleasure. Now try taking piano lessons, and suddenly the piano comes alive and brings forth magical sounds and rhythms that set your heart singing and your body swaying.

The same is true with your Rottweiler. At first you enjoy seeing him around the house. He does not do much with you other than to need food, water and exercise. Come to think of it, he does not bring you much joy, either. He is a big responsibility with a very small return. And often, he develops unacceptable behaviors that annoy and/or infuriate you, to say nothing of bad habits that may end up costing you great sums of money. Not a good thing!

Now train your Rottweiler. Enroll in an obedience class. Teach him good manners as you learn how and why he behaves the way he does. Find out how to communicate with your dog and how to recognize and understand his communications with you. Suddenly the dog takes on a new role in your life—he is smart, interesting, well behaved and fun to be with, and he demonstrates his bond of devotion to you daily. In other words, your Rottweiler does wonders for your ego because he constantly reminds you that you are not only his leader, you are his hero! Miraculous things have happened—you have a wonderful dog (even your family and friends have noticed the transformation!) and you feel good about yourself.

Those involved with teaching dog obedience and counseling owners about their dogs' behavior have discovered some interesting

Obedience training your Rottweiler is an absolute necessity. This dog knows the house rules and waits patiently by the door.

ATTENTION!
Your dog is actually training you at the same time you are training him. Dogs do things to get attention. They usually repeat whatever succeeds in getting your attention.

facts about dog ownership. For example, training dogs when they are puppies results in the highest rate of success in developing well-mannered and well-adjusted adult dogs. Training an older dog, say from six months to six years of age, can produce almost equal results, providing that the owner accepts the dog's slower rate of learning capability and is willing to work patiently to help the dog succeed at developing to his fullest potential. Unfortunately, the patience factor is what many owners of untrained adult dogs lack, so they do not persist until their dogs are successful at learning particular behaviors.

Training a puppy, for example, aged 8 to 16 weeks (20 weeks at the most) is like working with a dry sponge in a pool of water. The pup soaks up whatever you show him and constantly looks for more things to do and learn. At this early age, his body is not yet producing hormones, and therein lies the reason for such a high rate of success. Without hormones, he is focused on his owners and not particularly interested in investi-

gating other places, dogs, people, etc. You are his leader: his provider of food, water, shelter and security. Therefore, he latches onto you and wants to stay close. He will usually follow you from room to room, will not let you out of his sight when you are outdoors with him and will respond in like manner to the people and animals you encounter. If, for example, you greet a friend warmly, he will be happy to greet the person as well. If, however, you are hesitant or anxious about the approach of a stranger, the pup will respond accordingly.

Once the puppy begins to produce hormones, his natural curiosity emerges and he begins to investigate the world around him. It is at that time when you may notice that the untrained dog begins to wander away from you and even ignore your commands to stay close. When this behavior becomes a problem, the owner has two choices: get rid of the dog or train him. It is strongly urged that you choose the latter option.

Occasionally there are no classes available within a reasonable distance from the owner's home. Sometimes there are classes available but the tuition is too costly. Whatever the circumstances, the solution to training your Rottie without formal lessons lies within the pages of this book.

This chapter is devoted to helping you train your Rottweiler at home. If the recommended procedures are followed faithfully, you may expect positive results that will prove rewarding to both you and your dog.

Whether your Rottweiler is a puppy or a mature adult, the methods of teaching and the techniques we use in training basic behaviors are the same. After all, no dog, whether puppy or adult, likes harsh or inhumane methods. All creatures, however, respond favorably to gentle motivational methods and sincere praise and encouragement. Now let us get started.

HOUSEBREAKING

You can train a puppy to relieve himself wherever you choose. For example, city dwellers often train their puppies to relieve themselves while out walking because large plots of grass are not readily available. Suburbanites, on the other hand, usually have yards to accommodate their dogs' needs. In both cases, picking up the dog's droppings is critical and in public

The great outdoors means unexplored territory for a pup—keep a close eye on him as he familiarizes himself with the yard.

areas it is required by law.

Outdoor training includes such surfaces as grass, dirt and cement. Indoor training usually means training your dog to newspaper. When deciding on the surface and location that you will want your Rottweiler to use, be sure it is going to be permanent. Training your dog to grass and then changing your mind two months later is extremely difficult for both dog and owner.

Next, choose the command you will use each and every time you want your puppy to void. "Go hurry up" and "Go make" are examples of commands commonly used by dog owners. Get in the habit of asking the puppy, "Do you want to go hurry up?" (or whatever your chosen relief command is) before you take him out. That way, when he becomes an adult, you will be able to determine if he wants to go out when you ask him. A confirmation will be signs of interest, such as wagging his tail, watching you intently, going to the door, etc.

FAMILY TIES

If you have other pets in the home and/or interact often with the pets of friends and other family members, your pup will respond to those pets in much the same manner as you do. It is only when you show fear of or resentment toward another animal that he will act fearful or unfriendly.

OBEDIENCE SCHOOL

A basic obedience beginner's class usually lasts for six to eight weeks. Dog and owner attend an hour-long lesson once a week and practice for a few minutes, several times a day, each day at home. If done properly, the whole procedure will result in a well-mannered dog and an owner who delights in living with a pet that is eager to please and enjoys doing things with his owner.

PUPPY'S NEEDS

The puppy needs to relieve himself after play periods, after each meal, after he has been sleeping and any time he indicates that he is looking for a place to urinate or defecate.

The urinary and intestinal tract muscles of very young puppies are not fully developed. Therefore, like human babies, puppies need to relieve themselves frequently. Take your puppy out often—every hour for an eight-week-old, for example. The older the puppy, the less often he will need to relieve himself. Finally, as a mature healthy adult, he will require only three to five relief trips per day.

HOUSING

Since the types of housing and control you provide for your puppy have a direct relationship on the success of house-training, we consider the various aspects of both before we begin training.

Bringing a new puppy home and turning him loose in your house can be compared to turning a child loose in a sports arena and telling the child that the place is all his! The sheer enormity of the place would be too much for him to handle.

Instead, offer the puppy clearly defined areas where he can play, sleep, eat and live. A room of the house where the family gathers is the most obvious choice. Puppies are social animals and need to feel a part of the pack right from the start. Hearing your voice, watching you while you are doing things and smelling you nearby are all positive reinforcers that he is now a member of your pack. Usually a family room, the kitchen or a nearby adjoining breakfast nook is ideal for providing safety and security for both puppy and owner.

Within that room there should be a smaller area that the puppy can call his own. A cubbyhole, a dog crate or a partitioned-off (not boarded!) corner from which he can view the activities of his new family will be fine. The size of the area or crate is the key factor here. The area must be large enough for the puppy to lie down and stretch out as well as stand up without

Canine Development Schedule

It is important to understand how and at what age a puppy develops into adulthood. If you are a puppy owner, consult the following Canine Development Schedule to determine the stage of development your Rottweiler puppy is currently experiencing. This knowledge will help you as you work with the puppy in the weeks and months ahead.

Period	Age	Characteristics
FIRST TO THIRD	**BIRTH TO SEVEN WEEKS**	Puppy needs food, sleep and warmth, and responds to simple and gentle touching. Needs mother for security and disciplining. Needs littermates for learning and interacting with other dogs. Pup learns to function within a pack and learns pack order of dominance. Begin socializing with adults and children for short periods. Begins to become aware of his environment.
FOURTH	**EIGHT TO TWELVE WEEKS**	Brain is fully developed. Needs socializing with outside world. Remove from mother and littermates. Needs to change from canine pack to human pack. Human dominance necessary. Fear period occurs between 8 and 16 weeks. Avoid fright and pain.
FIFTH	**THIRTEEN TO SIXTEEN WEEKS**	Training and formal obedience should begin. Less association with other dogs, more with people, places, situations. Period will pass easily if you remember this is pup's change-to-adolescence time. Be firm and fair. Flight instinct prominent. Permissiveness and over-disciplining can do permanent damage. Praise for good behavior.
JUVENILE	**FOUR TO EIGHT MONTHS**	Another fear period about 7 to 8 months of age. It passes quickly, but be cautious of fright and pain. Sexual maturity reached. Dominant traits established. Dog should understand sit, down, come and stay by now.

NOTE: THESE ARE APPROXIMATE TIME FRAMES. ALLOW FOR INDIVIDUAL DIFFERENCES IN PUPPIES.

rubbing his head on the top, yet small enough so that he cannot relieve himself at one end and sleep at the other without coming into contact with his droppings.

Dogs are, by nature, clean animals and will not remain close to their relief areas unless forced to do so. In those cases, they then become dirty dogs and usually remain that way for life.

The crate should be lined with a clean towel or mat and offer one toy, no more. Do not put food or water in the crate, as eating and drinking will activate his digestive processes and ultimately defeat your purpose as well as make the puppy very uncomfortable as he attempts to "hold it."

CONTROL

By *control*, we mean helping the puppy to create a lifestyle pattern that will be compatible to that of his human pack (*you!*). Just as we guide little children to learn our way of life, we must show the

A thirsty dog will find a way to quench his thirst; however, a preferable alternative to the fish pond is a clean water bowl with fresh water.

> **HOUSE-TRAINING TIP**
> Most of all, be consistent. Always take your dog to the same location, always use the same command and always have the dog on leash when he is in his relief area, unless a fenced-in yard is available.
>
> By following the Success Method, your puppy will be completely house-broken by the time his muscle and brain development reach maturity. Keep in mind that small breeds usually mature faster than large breeds, but all puppies should be trained by six months of age.

puppy when it is time to play, eat, sleep, exercise and even entertain himself.

Your puppy should always sleep in his crate. He should also learn that, during times of household confusion and excessive human activity such as at breakfast when family members are preparing for the day, he can play by himself in relative safety and comfort in his crate. Each time you leave the puppy alone, he should be crated. Puppies are chewers. They cannot tell the difference between dog bones and lamp cords, television wires, shoes, table legs, etc. Chewing into a television wire, for example, can be fatal to the puppy, while a shorted wire can start a fire in the house.

If the puppy chews on the arm of the chair when he is alone, you will probably discipline him angrily when you get home. Thus, he makes the association that your coming home means he is going to be punished. (He will not remember chewing up the chair and is incapable of making the association of the discipline with his naughty deed.)

Times of excitement, such as family parties, visits, etc., can be fun for the puppy, providing he can view the activities from the security of his crate. He is not underfoot and he is not being fed all sorts of tidbits that will probably cause him stomach distress, yet he still feels a part of the fun.

SCHEDULE

As stated earlier, a puppy should be taken to his relief area each time he is released from his crate, after meals, after play sessions, when he first awakens in the morning (at age 8 weeks, this can mean 5 a.m.!) and whenever he indicates by circling or sniffing busily that he needs to urinate or defecate. For a puppy less than ten weeks of age, a routine of taking him out every hour is necessary. As the puppy grows, he will be able to wait for longer periods of time.

Keep trips to his relief area short. Stay no more than five or six minutes and then return to the house. If he goes during that time, praise him lavishly and take him indoors immediately. If he does not, but he has an accident when you go back indoors, pick him up immediately, say "No! No!" and return to his relief area. Wait a few minutes, then return to the house again. *Never* hit a puppy or put his face in urine or excrement when he has an accident!

Once indoors, put the puppy in his crate until you have had time to clean up his accident. Then release him to the family area and watch him more closely than before. Chances are, his accident was a result of your not picking up his signal or waiting too long before offering him the opportunity to relieve himself. *Never* hold a grudge against the puppy for accidents.

Let the puppy learn that going outdoors means it is time to relieve himself, not play. Once trained, he will be able to play indoors and out and still differentiate between the times for play

---

THE CLEAN LIFE

By providing sleeping and resting quarters that fit the dog, and offering frequent opportunities to relieve himself outside his quarters, the puppy quickly learns that the outdoors (or the newspaper if you are training him to paper) is the place to go when he needs to urinate or defecate. It also reinforces his innate desire to keep his sleeping quarters clean. This, in turn, helps develop the muscle control that will eventually produce a dog with clean living habits.

versus the times for relief.

Help him develop regular hours for naps, being alone, playing by himself and just resting, all in his crate. Encourage him to entertain himself while you are busy with your activities. Let him learn that having you near is comforting, but it is not your main purpose in life to provide him with undivided attention.

Each time you put a puppy in

THE SUCCESS METHOD

Success that comes by luck is usually short-lived. Success that comes by well-thought-out proven methods is often more easily achieved and permanent. This is the Success Method. It is designed to give you, the puppy owner, a simple yet proven way to help your puppy develop clean living habits and a feeling of security in his new environment.

6 Steps to Successful Crate Training

1 Tell the puppy "Crate time!" and place him in the crate with a small treat (a piece of cheese or half of a biscuit). Let him stay in the crate for five minutes while you are in the same room. Then release him and praise lavishly. Never release him when he is fussing. Wait until he is quiet before you let him out.

2 Repeat Step 1 several times a day.

3 The next day, place the puppy in the crate as before. Let him stay there for ten minutes. Do this several times.

4 Continue building time in five-minute increments until the puppy stays in his crate for 30 minutes with you in the room. Always take him to his relief area after prolonged periods in his crate.

5 Now go back to Step 1 and let the puppy stay in his crate for five minutes, this time while you are out of the room.

6 Once again, build crate time in five-minute increments with you out of the room. When the puppy will stay willingly in his crate (he may even fall asleep!) for 30 minutes with you out of the room, he will be ready to stay in it for several hours at a time.

his crate, tell him "Crate time" (or whatever command you choose). Soon, he will run to his crate when he hears you say those words.

In the beginning of his training, do not leave him in his crate for prolonged periods of time except during the night when everyone is sleeping. Make his experience with his crate a pleasant one and, as an adult, he will love his crate and willingly stay in it for several hours. There are millions of people who go to work every day and leave their adult dogs crated while they are away. The dogs accept this as their lifestyle and look forward to "crate time."

Crate training provides safety for you, the puppy and the home. It also provides the puppy with a feeling of security, and that helps the puppy achieve self-confidence and clean habits.

Remember that one of the primary ingredients in house-training your puppy is control. Regardless of your lifestyle, there will always be occasions when you will need to have a place where your dog can stay and be happy and safe. Crate training is the answer for now and in the future.

In conclusion, a few key elements are really all you need for a successful house- and crate-training method—consistency, frequency, praise, control and supervision. By following these procedures with a normal, healthy puppy, you and the puppy will soon be past the stage of accidents and ready to move on to a full and rewarding life together.

ROLES OF DISCIPLINE, REWARD AND PUNISHMENT

Discipline, training one to act in accordance with rules, brings order to life. It is as simple as that. Without discipline, particularly in a group society, chaos reigns supreme and the group will eventually perish. Humans and canines are social animals and need some form of discipline in order to function effectively. They must procure food, reproduce to keep the species going and protect their home base and their young. If there were no discipline in the lives of social animals, they would

PAPER CAPER

Never line your pup's sleeping area with newspaper. Puppy litters are usually raised on newspaper and, once in your home, the puppy will immediately associate newspaper with voiding. Never put newspaper on any floor while house-training, as this will only confuse the puppy. If you are paper-training him, use paper in his designated relief area only. Finally, restrict water intake after evening meals. Offer a few licks at a time—never let a young puppy gulp water after meals.

Your local pet shop will have an assortment of collars. Get the one that best suits your needs. A chain collar should only be used by someone who has been instructed in its proper use.

eventually die from starvation and/or predation by other stronger animals.

In the case of domestic canines, dogs need discipline in their lives in order to understand how their pack (you and other family members) functions and how they must act in order to survive.

A large humane society in a highly populated area recently surveyed dog owners regarding their satisfaction with their relationships with their dogs. People who had trained their dogs were 75% more satisfied with their pets than those who had never trained their dogs.

Dr. Edward Thorndike, a noted psychologist, established *Thorndike's Theory of Learning*, which states that a behavior that results in a pleasant event tends to be repeated. Likewise, a behavior that results in an unpleasant event tends not to be repeated. It is this theory on which training methods are based today. For example, if you manipulate a dog to perform a specific behavior and reward him for doing it, he is likely to do it again because he enjoyed the end result.

Occasionally, punishment, a penalty inflicted for an offense, is necessary. The best type of punishment often comes from an outside source. For example, a child is told not to touch the stove because he may get burned. He disobeys and touches the stove. In doing so, he receives a burn. From that time on, he respects the heat of the stove and avoids contact with it. Therefore, a behavior that results in an unpleasant event tends not to be repeated.

A good example of a dog learning the hard way is the dog who chases the house cat. He is told many times to leave the cat alone, yet he persists in teasing the cat. Then, one day he begins chasing the cat but the cat turns

PLAN TO PLAY

The puppy should also have regular play and exercise sessions when he is with you or a family member. Exercise for a very young puppy can consist of a short walk around the house or yard. Playing can include fetching games with a large ball or a special toy. (All puppies teethe and need soft things upon which to chew.) Remember to restrict play periods to indoors within his living area (the family room, for example) until he is completely house-trained.

and swipes a claw across the dog's face, leaving him with a painful gash on his nose. The final result is that the dog stops chasing the cat.

TRAINING EQUIPMENT

COLLAR

A simple buckle collar, usually constructed of strong nylon or leather is fine for most dogs. A Rottweiler who pulls mightily on the leash may require a chain choke collar. A chain choke collar should never be left on the dog when not training.

LEASH

A 6-foot leash is recommended, preferably made of leather, nylon or heavy cloth. Obviously a Rottie requires a strong leash, given the dog's considerable size and strength.

TREATS

Have a bag of treats on hand. Something nutritious and easy to swallow works best; use a soft treat, a chunk of cheese or a piece of cooked chicken rather than a dry biscuit. By the time the dog gets done chewing a dry treat, he will forget why he is being rewarded in the first place! Incidentally, food rewards will not teach a dog to beg at the table—the only way to teach a dog to beg at the table is to give him food from the table. In training, rewarding

the dog with a food treat away from the table will help him associate praise and the treats with learning new behaviors that obviously please his owner.

TRAINING BEGINS: ASK THE DOG A QUESTION

In order to teach your dog anything, you must first get his attention. After all, he cannot learn anything if he is looking away from you with his mind on something else.

To get his attention, ask him "School?" and immediately walk over to him and give him a treat as you tell him "Good dog." Wait a minute or two and repeat the routine, this time with a treat in your hand as you approach the dog to within a foot of him. Do not go directly to him, but stop about a foot short of him and hold out the treat as you ask "School?" He will see you approaching with a treat in your hand and most likely begin walking toward you. As you

If your Rottweiler knows you have a treat in your hand, he won't take his eyes off you.

PRACTICE MAKES PERFECT!

- Have training lessons with your dog every day in several short segments—three to five times a day for a few minutes at a time is ideal.
- Do not have long practice sessions. The dog will become easily bored.
- Never practice when you are tired, ill, worried or in an otherwise negative mood. This will transmit to the dog and may have an adverse effect on his performance.

Think fun, short and above all *positive*! End each session on a high note, rather than a failed exercise, and make sure to give a lot of praise. Enjoy the training and help your dog enjoy it, too.

meet, give him the treat and praise again.

The third time, ask the question, have a treat in your hand and walk only a short distance toward the dog so that he must walk almost all the way to you. As he reaches you, give him the treat and praise again.

By this time, the dog will probably be getting the idea that if he pays attention to you, especially when you ask that question, it will pay off in treats and fun activities for him. In other words, he learns that "school" means doing fun things with you that result in treats and positive attention for him.

Remember that the dog does not understand your verbal language, he only recognizes sounds. Your question translates to a series of sounds for him, and those sounds become the signal to go to you and pay attention; if he does, he will get to interact with you plus receive treats and praise.

THE BASIC COMMANDS

TEACHING SIT

Now that you have the dog's attention, hold the leash in your left hand and the food treat in your right. Place your food hand at the dog's nose and let him lick the treat but not take it from you. Say "Sit" and slowly raise your food hand from in front of the dog's nose up over his head so that he is looking at the ceiling. As he bends his head upward, he will have to bend his knees to maintain his balance. As he bends his knees, he will assume a sit position. At that point, release the food treat and praise lavishly with comments such as "Good dog! Good sit!," etc. Remember to always praise enthusiastically, because dogs relish verbal praise from their owners and feel so proud of themselves whenever they accomplish a behavior.

You will not use food forever in getting the dog to obey your commands. Food is only used to teach new behaviors, and once the dog knows what you want when you give a specific command, you will wean him off of the food treats but still maintain the verbal praise. After all, you will always have your voice with you, but

In order to teach your Rottweiler, you must make eye contact and hold his attention.

there will be many times when you have no food rewards yet you expect the dog to obey.

TEACHING DOWN

Teaching the down exercise is easy when you understand how the dog perceives the down position, and it is very difficult when you do not. In addition, teaching the down exercise using the wrong method can sometimes make the dog develop such a fear of the down that he either runs away when you say "Down" or he attempts to bite the person who tries to force him down.

Have the dog sit close alongside your left leg, facing in the same direction as you are. Hold the leash in your left hand and a food treat in your right. Now place your left hand lightly on the top of the dog's shoulders where they

LANGUAGE BARRIER

Dogs do not understand our language and have to rely on tone of voice more than just words or sound. They can be trained to react to a certain sound, at a certain volume. If you say "No, Oliver" in a very soft, pleasant voice, it will not have the same meaning as "No, Oliver!!" when you raise your voice. You should never use the dog's name during a reprimand, just the command "No!" You never want the dog to associate his name with a negative experience or reprimand.

meet above the spinal cord. Do not push down on the dog's shoulders; simply rest your left hand there so you can guide the dog to lie down close to your left leg rather than to swing away from your side when he drops.

Now place the food hand at the dog's nose, say "Down" very softly (almost a whisper) and slowly lower the food hand to the dog's front feet. When the food hand reaches the floor, begin moving it forward along the floor in front of the dog. Keep talking softly to the dog, saying things like, "Do you want this treat? You

Start heel training with your dog sitting close to your left leg before taking a step forward.

can do this, good dog." Your reassuring tone of voice will help calm the dog as he tries to follow the food hand in order to get the treat.

When the dog's elbows touch the floor, release the food and praise softly. Try to get the dog to maintain that down position for several seconds before you let him sit up again. The goal here is to get the dog to settle down and not feel threatened in the down position.

TEACHING STAY

It is easy to teach the dog to stay in either a sit or a down position. Again, we use food and praise during the teaching process as we help the dog to understand exactly what it is that we are expecting him to do.

To teach the sit/stay, start with the dog sitting on your left side as before and hold the leash in your left hand. Have a food treat in your right hand and place your food hand at the dog's nose. Say "Stay" and step out on your right foot to stand directly in front of the dog, toe to toe, as he licks and nibbles the treat. Be sure to keep his head facing upward to maintain the sit position. Count to five and then swing around to stand next to the dog again with him on your left. As soon as you get back to the original position, release the food and praise lavishly.

To teach the down/stay, do the down as previously described. As soon as the dog lies down, say

"Stay" and step out on your right foot just as you did in the sit/stay. Count to five and then return to stand beside the dog with him on your left side. Release the treat and praise as always.

Within a week or ten days, you can begin to add a bit of distance between you and your dog when you leave him. When you do, use your left hand open with the palm facing the dog as a stay signal, much the same as the hand signal a police officer uses to stop traffic at an intersection. Hold the food treat in your right hand as before, but this time the food is not touching the dog's nose. He will watch the food hand and quickly learn that he is going to get that treat as soon as you return to his side.

When you can stand 1 yard away from your dog for 30 seconds, you can then begin building time and distance in both stays. Eventually, the dog can be expected to remain in the stay position for prolonged periods of time until you return to him or call him to you. Always praise lavishly when he stays.

TEACHING COME

If you make teaching "come" a fun experience, you should never have a student that does not love the game or that fails to come when called. The secret, it seems, is never to teach the word "come."

At times when an owner most wants his dog to come when called, the owner is likely upset or anxious and he allows these feelings to come through in the tone of his voice when he calls his dog. Hearing that desperation in his owner's voice, the dog fears the results of going to him and therefore either disobeys outright or runs in the opposite direction. The secret, therefore, is to teach the dog a game and, when you want him to come to you, simply play the game. It is practically a no-fail solution!

In teaching the down, give the dog a treat when his elbows touch the grass.

Use praise and patience to train your Rottweiler to stay in the down position.

To begin, have several members of your family take a few food treats and each go into a different room in the house. Take turns calling the dog, and each person should celebrate the dog's finding him with a treat and lots of happy praise. When a person calls the dog, he is actually inviting the dog to find him and get a treat as a reward for "winning."

A few turns of the "Where are you?" game and the dog will figure out that everyone is playing the game and that each person has a big celebration awaiting his success at locating them. Once he learns to love the game, simply calling out "Where are you?" will bring the dog running from wher-

ever he is when he hears that all-important question.

The come command is recognized as one of the most important things to teach a dog, so it is interesting to note that there are trainers who work with thousands of dogs and never teach the actual word "come." Yet these dogs will race to respond to a person who uses the dog's name followed by "Where are you?" In one instance, for example, a woman has a nine-year-old companion dog who went blind, but who never fails to locate her owner when asked, "Where are you?"

Children particularly love to play this game with their dogs. Children can hide in smaller

"WHERE ARE YOU?"
When calling the dog, do not say "Come." Say things like, "Rover, where are you? See if you can find me! I have a biscuit for you!" Keep up a constant line of chatter with coaxing sounds and frequent questions such as, "Where are you?" The dog will learn to follow the sound of your voice to locate you and receive his reward.

A group demonstration given by some well-trained Rottweilers and their handlers.

places like a shower or bathtub, behind a bed or under a table. The dog needs to work a little bit harder to find these hiding places but, when he does, he loves to celebrate with a treat and a tussle with a favorite youngster.

TEACHING HEEL

Heeling means that the dog walks beside the owner without pulling. It takes time and patience on the owner's part to succeed at teaching the dog that he (the owner) will not proceed unless the dog is walking calmly beside him. Pulling out ahead on the leash is definitely not acceptable.

Begin with holding the leash in your left hand as the dog sits beside your left leg. Hold the loop end of the leash in your right hand but keep your left hand short on the leash so it keeps the dog in close next to you.

Say "Heel" and step forward on your left foot. Keep the dog close to you and take three steps. Stop and have the dog sit next to you in what we now call the heel position. Praise verbally, but do not touch the dog. Hesitate a moment and begin again with "Heel," taking three steps and stopping, at which point the dog is told to sit again.

Your goal here is to have the

REAP THE REWARDS

If you start with a normal, healthy dog and give him time, patience and some carefully executed lessons, you will reap the rewards of that training for the life of the dog. And what a life it will be! The two of you will find immeasurable pleasure in the companionship you have built together with love, respect and understanding.

dog walk those three steps without pulling on the leash. When he will walk calmly beside you for three steps without pulling, increase the number of steps you take to five. When he will walk politely beside you while you take five steps, you can increase the length of your walk to ten steps. Keep increasing the length of your stroll until the dog will walk quietly beside you without pulling as long as you want him to heel. When you stop

TUG OF WALK?
If you begin teaching the heel by taking long walks and letting the dog pull you along, he misinterprets this action as an acceptable form of taking a walk. When you pull back on the leash to counteract his pulling, he reads that tug as a signal to pull even harder!

Teaching your Rottweiler to come is absolutely necessary.

heeling, indicate to the dog that the exercise is over by verbally praising as you pet him and say "OK, good dog." The "OK" is used as a release word, meaning that the exercise is finished and the dog is free to relax.

If you are dealing with a dog who insists on pulling you around, simply "put on your brakes" and stand your ground until the dog realizes that the two of you are not going anywhere until he is beside you and moving at your pace, not his. It may take some time just standing there to convince the dog that you are the leader and you will be the one to decide on the direction and speed of your travel.

Each time the dog looks up at you or slows down to give a slack leash between the two of you, quietly praise him and say, "Good heel. Good dog." Eventually, the dog will begin to respond and within a few days he will be walking politely beside you without pulling on the leash. At first, the training sessions should be kept

In training to heel, gradually increase the number of steps you can take with your Rottweiler without his pulling on the leash.

short and very positive; soon the dog will be able to walk nicely with you for increasingly longer distances. Remember also to give the dog free time and the opportunity to run and play when you are done with heel practice.

WEANING OFF FOOD IN TRAINING

Food is used in training new behaviors, yet once the dog understands what behavior goes with a specific command, it is time to start weaning him off the food treats. At first, give a treat after each exercise. Then, start to give a treat only after every other exer-

cise. Mix up the times when you offer a food reward and the times when you only offer praise so that the dog will never know when he is going to receive both food and praise and when he is going to receive only praise. This is called a variable ratio reward system and it proves successful because there is always the chance that the owner will produce a treat, so the dog never stops trying for that reward. No matter what, *always* give verbal praise.

OBEDIENCE CLASSES

As previously discussed, it is a good idea to enroll in an obedience class if one is available in your area. If yours is a show pup, handling classes are a smart investment. Many areas have dog clubs that offer basic obedience training as well as preparatory classes for obedience competition. There are also local dog trainers who offer similar classes.

At obedience trials, dogs can earn titles at various levels of competition. The beginning levels of competition include basic behaviors such as sit, down, heel, etc. The more advanced levels of competition include jumping, retrieving, scent discrimination and signal work. The advanced

> **KEEP SMILING**
> Never train your dog, puppy or adult, when you are angry or in a sour mood. Dogs are very sensitive to human feelings, especially anger, and if your dog senses that you are angry or upset, he will connect your anger with his training and learn to resent or fear his training sessions.

levels require a dog and owner to put a lot of time and effort into their training; the titles that can be earned at these levels of competition are very prestigious.

OTHER ACTIVITIES FOR LIFE
Whether a dog is trained in the structured environment of a class or alone with his owner at home, there are many activities that can bring fun and rewards to both owner and dog once they have mastered basic control.

Teaching the dog to help out around the home, in the yard or on the farm provides great satisfaction to both dog and owner. In addition, the dog's help makes life a little easier for his owner and raises his stature as a valued companion to his family. It helps give the dog a purpose; it helps to keep his mind occupied and provides an outlet for his energy.

Backpacking is an exciting and healthful activity that the dog can be taught without assistance from more than his owner. The exercise

Walking your Rottweiler should be a pleasant experience. It should never be a battle of who is walking whom.

of walking and climbing is good for man and dog alike, and the bond that they develop together is priceless.

If you are interested in participating in organized competition with your Rottweiler, there are other activities other than obedience in which you and your dog can become involved. Agility is a popular and fun sport where dogs run through an obstacle course that includes various jumps, tunnels and other exercises to test the dog's speed and coordination. The owners often run through the course beside their dogs to give commands and to guide them through the course. Although competitive, the focus is on fun—it's fun to do and fun to watch, as well as great exercise.

As a Rottweiler owner, you have the opportunity to participate in Schutzhund competition if you

Once you have trained your Rottweiler to sit reliably, you can teach him the sit-stay quite readily.

so choose. Schutzhund originated in Germany as a test to determine the best quality Rottweilers to be used for breeding stock. It is now used as a way to evaluate working ability and temperament, and some Rottweiler owners choose to train their dogs in Schutzhund tests. There are three levels of Schutzhund, SchH. I, SchH. II and SchH. III, each level being progressively more difficult to complete successfully. Each level consists of training, obedience and protection phases. Training for Schutzhund is intense and must be practiced consistently to keep the dog keen. The experience of Schutzhund training is very rewarding for dog and owner, and the Rottweiler's tractability is well suited for this type of serious training.

A BORN PRODIGY

Occasionally, a dog and owner who have not attended formal classes have been able to earn entry-level titles by obtaining competition rules and regulations from a local kennel club and practicing on their own to a degree of perfection. Obtaining the higher level titles, however, almost always requires extensive training under the tutelage of experienced instructors. In addition, the more difficult levels require more specialized equipment whereas the lower levels do not.

MEDICAL PROBLEMS
MOST FREQUENTLY SEEN IN ROTTWEILERS

Condition	Age Affected	Cause	Area Affected
Acral Lick Granuloma	Any age, males	Unknown	Legs
Aortic Stenosis	Young pups	Congenital	Heart
Degenerative Myelopathy	1 to 3 years	Hereditary	Spinal cord/brain
Elbow Dysplasia	4 to 7 mos	Congenital	Elbow joint
Gastric Dilatation (Bloat)	Older dogs	Swallowing air	Stomach
Hip Dysplasia	By 2 years	Congenital	Hip joint
Hypothyroidism	1 to 3 years	Lymphocytic thyroiditis	Endocrine system
Osteochondrosis	4 to 7 months	Improper nutrition/exercise	Cartilage
Progressive Retinal Atrophy	Any age	Hereditary	Retinal tissue/eyes
Retinal Dysplasia	Birth	Hereditary	Retina
Von Willebrand's Disease	Birth	Congenital	Blood

Health Care of Your Rottweiler

Dogs, being mammals like human beings, suffer from many of the same physical illnesses as people. They might even share many of the same psychological problems. Since people usually know more about human diseases than canine maladies, many of the terms used in this chapter will be the familiar terms, not necessarily those used by veterinarians. We'll still use the term *x-ray*, instead of the more acceptable term *radiograph*. We will also use the familiar term *symptoms* even though dogs don't have symptoms, dogs have *clinical signs. Symptoms* are actually verbal descriptions of the patient's feelings, and since dogs can't speak, we have to look for clinical signs.

As a general rule, medicine is *practiced*. That term is not arbitrary. Medicine is a constantly changing art as we learn more and more about genetics, electronic aids (like CAT scans and MRIs) and other advances. There are many dog maladies, like canine hip dysplasia, which are not univer-

sally treated in the same manner. Some vets opt for surgery more often than others.

SELECTING A QUALIFIED VET

Your selection of a veterinarian should be based not only upon his personality and ability with large-breed dogs but also upon his convenience to your home. You want a vet who is close as you might have emergencies or multiple visits for treatments. You want a vet who has services that you might require such as microchipping or boarding facilities, who makes sophisticated pet supplies available and who has a good reputation for ability and

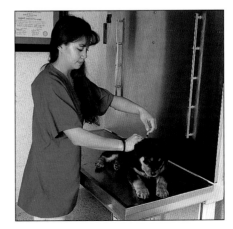

Select your veterinarian based on proximity to your home and recommendations from other dog owners.

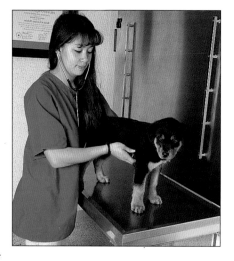

such is required for show purposes. When the problem affecting your dog is serious, it is not unusual or impudent to get another medical opinion. You might also want to compare costs between several veterinarians. Sophisticated health care and veterinary services can be very costly. Don't be bashful about discussing costs with your veterinarian or his staff. It is not infrequent that important decisions are based upon financial considerations.

responsiveness. There is nothing more frustrating than having to wait a day or more to get a response from a veterinarian.

All veterinarians are licensed and their diplomas and/or certificates should be displayed in their waiting rooms. There are, however, many veterinary specialties which usually require further studies and internships. There are specialists in heart problems (veterinary cardiologists), skin problems (veterinary dermatologists), teeth and gum problems (veterinary dentists), eye problems (veterinary ophthalmologists) and x-rays (veterinary radiologists), and surgeons who have specialties in bones, muscles or certain organs. Most veterinarians do routine surgery such as neutering, stitching up wounds and docking tails for those breeds in which

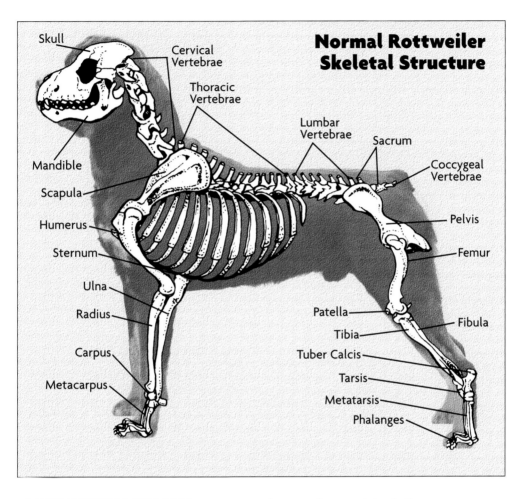

Skull
Cervical Vertebrae
Thoracic Vertebrae
Lumbar Vertebrae
Sacrum

Normal Rottweiler Skeletal Structure

Mandible
Scapula
Humerus
Sternum
Ulna
Radius
Carpus
Metacarpus

Coccygeal Vertebrae
Pelvis
Femur
Patella
Fibula
Tibia
Tuber Calcis
Tarsis
Metatarsis
Phalanges

PREVENTATIVE MEDICINE

It is much easier, less costly and more effective to practice preventative medicine than to fight bouts of illness and disease. Properly bred puppies come from parents that were selected based upon their genetic-disease profiles. Their dam should have been vaccinated, free of all internal and external parasites and properly nourished. For these reasons, a visit to the vet who cared for the dam is recommended. The dam can pass on disease resistance to her puppies. This resistance can last for eight to ten weeks. She can also pass on parasites and many infections. That's why you should learn as much about the dam's health as possible.

AFTER WEANING TO FIVE MONTHS OLD

Puppies should be weaned by the time they are about two months old. A puppy that remains for at least eight weeks with his mother and littermates usually adapts better to other dogs and people later in his life.

In every case, you should have your newly acquired puppy examined by a vet immediately. Vaccination programs usually begin when the puppy is very young.

The puppy will have his teeth examined, have his skeletal conformation checked and have his general health checked prior to certification by the vet. Many puppies have problems with their knee caps, cataracts and other eye problems, heart murmurs and undescended testicles. They may also have person-

DEWORMING

Ridding your puppy of worms is very important because they remove the nutrients that a growing puppy needs and certain worms that puppies carry, such as tapeworms and roundworms, can also infect humans.

Breeders initiate deworming programs at or about four weeks of age. The routine is repeated every two or three weeks until the puppy is three months old. The breeder from whom you obtained your puppy should provide you with the complete details of the deworming program.

Your veterinarian can prescribe and monitor the rest of the deworming program for you. The usual program is treating the puppy every 15–20 days until the puppy is positively worm-free. It is advised that you only treat your puppy with drugs that are recommended professionally.

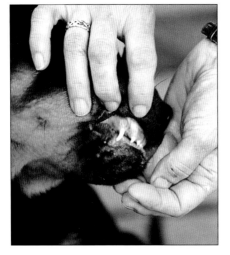

The vet will examine your puppy's developing bite to ensure that all teeth have properly erupted.

ality problems and your vet might have training in temperament evaluation.

VACCINATION SCHEDULING

Most vaccinations are given by injection and should only be done by a veterinarian. Both he and you should keep a record of the date of the injection, the identification of the vaccine and the amount given. The vaccination scheduling is based on a 15-day cycle. The first vaccinations should start when the puppy is

HEALTH AND VACCINATION SCHEDULE

Age in Weeks:	3rd	6th	8th	10th	12th	14th	16th	20-24th
Worm Control	✔	✔	✔	✔	✔	✔	✔	✔
Neutering								✔
Heartworm		✔						✔
Parvovirus		✔		✔		✔		✔
Distemper			✔		✔		✔	
Hepatitis			✔		✔		✔	
Leptospirosis		✔		✔		✔		
Parainfluenza		✔		✔		✔		
Dental Examination			✔					✔
Complete Physical			✔					✔
Temperament Testing			✔					
Coronavirus					✔			
Kennel Cough		✔						
Hip Dysplasia							✔	
Rabies								✔

Vaccinations are not instantly effective. It takes about two weeks for the dog's immune system to develop antibodies. Most vaccinations require annual booster shots. Your veterinarian should guide you in this regard.

6–8 weeks old, then 15 days later when he is 10–12 weeks of age and later when he is 14–16 weeks of age. Vaccinations should *never* be given without a 15-day lapse between injections.

Most vaccinations immunize your puppy against viruses. The usual vaccines contain immunizing doses of several different viruses such as distemper, parvovirus, parainfluenza and hepatitis. There are other vaccines available when the puppy is at risk. You should rely upon professional advice. This is especially true for the booster-shot program. Most vaccination programs require a booster when

KEEPING HER HEALTHY

Caring for the puppy starts before the puppy is born by keeping the dam healthy and well-nourished. When the puppy is about three weeks old, he must start his disease-control regimen. The first treatments will be for worms. Most puppies have worms, even if they have tested negative for worms. The test essentially is checking the stool specimens for the eggs of the worms. The worms continually shed eggs except during their dormant stage when they just rest in the tissues of the puppy. During this stage they don't shed eggs and are not evident during a routine examination.

the puppy is a year old, and once a year thereafter. In some cases, circumstances may require more or less frequent immunizations.

Kennel cough, more formally known as *tracheobronchitis*, is treated with a vaccine which is sprayed into the dog's nostrils.

The effectiveness of the parvovirus vaccination program can be tested to be certain that the vaccinations are protective. Your veterinarian will explain and manage all of these details.

FIVE MONTHS TO ONE YEAR OF AGE

By the time your puppy is five months old, he should have completed his vaccination program. During his physical examination, he should be evaluated for the common hip dysplasia plus other diseases of the joints. There are tests to assist in the prediction of these problems. Other tests can also be run, such as the parvovirus antibody titer, which can assess the effectiveness of the vaccination program.

Unless you intend to breed or show your dog, neutering the puppy at six months of age is recommended. Discuss this with your veterinarian.

By the time the potential show-quality Rottweiler is seven or eight months of age, he can be seriously evaluated for his

IDENTIFICATION

As Rottweiler puppies become more and more expensive, especially those puppies of high quality for showing and/or breeding, they have a greater chance of being stolen. The usual collar dog tag is, of course, easily removed. But there are two permanent techniques that are becoming widely utilized for identification.

The puppy microchip implantation involves the injection of a small microchip, about the size of a corn kernel, under the skin of the dog. If your dog shows up at a clinic or shelter, or is offered for resale under less than savory circumstances, it can be positively identified by the microchip. The microchip is scanned and a registry quickly identifies you as the owner. This is not only protection against theft, but should the dog run away or go chasing a varmint and get lost, you have a fair chance of getting it back.

Tattooing is done on various parts of the dog, from the belly to the cheeks. The number tattooed can be your telephone number or any other number that you can easily memorize. When professional dog thieves see a tattooed dog, they usually lose interest in it. For the safety of our Rottweilers, no laboratory facility or dog broker will accept a tattooed dog as stock. Both microchipping and tattooing can be done at your local veterinary clinic.

conformation to the standard, thus determining his show potential and his desirability as a sire (or a dam). If the puppy is not top-class and therefore is not a candidate for a serious breeding program, most professionals advise neutering the puppy. Neutering and spaying have proven to be extremely beneficial to both male and female puppies. Besides the obvious impossibility of pregnancy, it inhibits (but does not prevent) breast cancer in bitches and prostate cancer in male dogs.

Blood tests are performed for heartworm infestation and it is possible that your puppy will be placed on a preventative therapy that will prevent heartworm infection as well as control other internal parasites.

DOGS OLDER THAN ONE YEAR

Continue to visit the veterinarian at least once a year. There is no such disease as old age, but bodily functions do change with age, and the eyes and ears are no longer as efficient. Neither are the internal workings of the liver, kidneys and intestines. Proper dietary changes, recommended by your veterinarian, can make life more pleasant for the aging Rottweiler and you.

SKIN PROBLEMS IN ROTTWEILERS

Veterinarians are consulted by dog owners for skin problems more than any other group of diseases or maladies. Dogs' skin is almost as sensitive as human skin and both suffer from almost

ROUTINE CARE

A dental examination is in order when the dog is between six months and one year of age, and any permanent teeth that have erupted incorrectly can be corrected. It is important to begin a brushing regimen at home, using dental-care products designed for dogs, such as canine toothpaste and toothbrushes. Durable nylon and safe edible chews should be a part of your puppy's arsenal for good health, good teeth and pleasant breath. The vast majority of dogs three to four years old and older has diseases of their gums from lack of dental attention. Using the various types of dental chews can be very effective in controlling dental plaque.

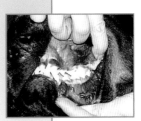

By the time your dog is a year old, you should have become very comfortable with your local veterinarian and have agreed on scheduled visits for booster vaccinations. Blood tests should now be taken regularly, for comparative purposes, for such variables as cholesterol and triglyceride levels, thyroid hormones, liver enzymes, blood cell counts, etc.

The eyes, ears, nose and throat should be examined regularly and annual cleaning of the teeth is a ritual. For teeth scaling, the dog must be anesthetized.

the same ailments (though the occurrence of acne in most breeds is rare!). For this reason, veterinary dermatology has developed into a specialty practiced by many veterinarians.

Since many skin problems have visual symptoms which are almost identical, it requires the skill of an experienced veterinary dermatologist to identify and cure many severe skin disorders. Simply put, if your dog is suffering from a skin disorder, seek professional assistance as quickly as possible. As with all diseases, the earlier a problem is identified and treated, the more likely it is that the cure will be successful.

Pet shops sell many treatments for skin problems. However, most of the treatments are simply directed at symptoms and not the underlying problem(s).

HEREDITARY SKIN DISORDERS
Veterinary dermatologists are currently researching a number of skin disorders that are believed to have a hereditary basis. These inherited diseases are transmitted by both parents, who appear (phenotypically) normal but have a recessive gene for the disease, meaning that they carry, but are not affected by, the disease. These diseases pose serious problems to breeders because in some instances there are no methods of identifying carriers. Often the secondary diseases associated with these skin conditions are even more debilitating than the skin disorders themselves, including cancers and respiratory problems.

Among the hereditary skin disorders, for which the mode of inheritance is known, are cutaneous asthenia (Ehlers-Danlos syndrome), sebaceous adenitis, cyclic hematopoiesis, dermatomyositis, IgA deficiency, color dilution alopecia and nodular dermatofibrosis. All inherited diseases must be diagnosed and treated by a veterinary specialist.

A SKUNKY PROBLEM
Have you noticed your dog dragging his rump along the floor? If so, it is likely that his anal sacs are impacted or possibly infected. The anal sacs are small pouches located on both sides of the anus under the skin and muscles. They are about the size and shape of a grape and contain a foul-smelling liquid. Their contents are usually emptied when the dog has a bowel movement but, if not emptied completely, they will impact, which will cause your dog much pain. Fortunately, your veterinarian can tend to this problem easily by draining the sacs for the dog. Be aware that your dog might also empty his anal sacs in cases of extreme fright.

PARASITE BITES

Many of us are allergic to mosquito bites. The bites itch, erupt and may even become infected. Dogs have the same reaction to fleas, ticks and/or mites. When you feel the prick of the mosquito when it bites you, you have a chance to kill it with your hand. Unfortunately, when your dog is bitten by a flea, tick or mite, it can only scratch it away or bite it. By the time the dog has been bitten, the parasite has done some of its damage. It may also have laid eggs to cause further problems in the near future. The itching from parasite bites is probably due to the saliva injected into the site when the parasite sucks the dog's blood.

Disease	What is it?	What causes it?	Symptoms
Leptospirosis	Severe disease that affects the internal organs; can be spread to people.	A bacterium, which is often carried by rodents, that enters through mucous membranes and spreads quickly throughout the body.	Range from fever, vomiting and loss of appetite in less severe cases to shock, irreversible kidney damage and possibly death in most severe cases.
Rabies	Potentially deadly virus that infects warm-blooded mammals.	Bite from a carrier of the virus, mainly wild animals.	1st stage: dog exhibits change in behavior, fear. 2nd stage: dog's behavior becomes more aggressive. 3rd stage: loss of coordination, trouble with bodily functions.
Parvovirus	Highly contagious virus, potentially deadly.	Ingestion of the virus, which is usually spread through the feces of infected dogs.	Most common: severe diarrhea. Also vomiting, fatigue, lack of appetite.
Kennel cough	Contagious respiratory infection.	Combination of types of bacteria and virus. Most common: *Bordetella bronchiseptica* bacteria and parainfluenza virus.	Chronic cough.
Distemper	Disease primarily affecting respiratory and nervous system.	Virus that is related to the human measles virus.	Mild symptoms such as fever, lack of appetite and mucous secretion progress to evidence of brain damage, "hard pad."
Hepatitis	Virus primarily affecting the liver.	Canine adenovirus type I (CAV-1). Enters system when dog breathes in particles.	Lesser symptoms include listlessness, diarrhea, vomiting. More severe symptoms include "blue-eye" (clumps of virus in eye).
Coronavirus	Virus resulting in digestive problems.	Virus is spread through infected dog's feces.	Stomach upset evidenced by lack of appetite, vomiting, diarrhea.

When a Rottweiler tirelessly licks a hot spot until the hair and skin have been removed, it is called acral lick granuloma. The cause of this syndrome is unknown.

SIMULATED MEDICAL CONDITION FOR EDUCATIONAL PURPOSES ONLY.

AUTO-IMMUNE SKIN CONDITIONS

Auto-immune skin conditions are commonly referred to as being allergic to yourself. Allergies, though, usually result in inflammatory reactions to an outside stimulus. Auto-immune diseases cause serious damage to the tissues that are involved.

The best known auto-immune disease is lupus. It affects people as well as dogs. The symptoms are very variable and may affect the kidneys, bones, blood chemistry and skin. It can be fatal to both dogs and humans, though it is not thought to be transmissible. It is usually successfully treated with cortisone, prednisone or similar corticosteroid, but extensive use of these drugs can have harmful side effects.

ACRAL LICK GRANULOMA

Rottweilers and other dogs about the same size have a very poorly understood syndrome called acral lick. The manifestation of the problem is the dog's tireless attack at a specific area of the body, almost always the legs. The dog licks so intensively that he removes the hair and skin, leaving an ugly, large wound. There is no absolute cure, but corticosteroids are the most common treatment.

AIRBORNE ALLERGIES

Just as humans have hay fever, rose fever and other fevers from which they suffer during the pollinating season, many dogs suffer from the same allergies. So when the pollen count is high, your dog might suffer. Don't expect them to sneeze and have a runny nose like humans do. Dogs react to pollen allergies the same way they react to fleas—they scratch and bite themselves.

FOOD INTOLERANCE

Food intolerance is the inability of the dog to completely digest certain foods. Puppies which may have done very well on their mother's milk may not do well on cow's milk. The result of this food intolerance may be loose bowels, passing gas and stomach pains. These are the only obvious symptoms of food intolerance and that makes diagnosis difficult.

Rottweilers are very susceptible to airborne pollen allergies.

Dogs, like humans, can be tested for allergens. Discuss the testing with your veterinary dermatologist.

FOOD ALLERGIES

Dogs are allergic to many foods that are best-sellers and highly recommended by breeders and veterinarians. Changing the brand of food that you buy may not eliminate the problem because the element of the food to which the dog is allergic may also be contained in the new brand.

Recognizing a food allergy is difficult. Humans vomit or have rashes when they eat a food to which they are allergic. Dogs neither vomit nor (usually) develop a rash. Instead they itch, scratch and bite, thus making the diagnosis extremely difficult. While pollen allergies and parasite bites are usually seasonal, food allergies are year-round problems.

TREATING FOOD PROBLEMS

Handling food allergies and food intolerance yourself is possible. Put your dog on a diet that he has never had. Obviously if he has never eaten this new food he can't have been allergic or intolerant of it. Start with a single ingredient that is *not* in the dog's diet at the present time. Ingredients like chopped beef or chicken

---

FAT OR FICTION?
The myth that dogs need extra fat in their diets can be harmful. Should your vet recommend extra fat, use safflower oil instead of animal oils. Safflower oil has been shown to be less likely to cause allergic reactions.

---

are common in dog's diets, so try something more exotic like fish, rabbit or some other source of quality protein. Keep the dog on this diet (with no additives) for a month. If the symptoms of food allergy or intolerance disappear, chances are that you have defined the cause.

Don't think that the single ingredient cured the problem. You still must find a suitable diet and ascertain which ingredient in the old diet was objectionable. This is most easily done by adding ingredients to the new diet one at a time until the problem is solved. Let the dog stay on the modified diet for a month before you add another ingredient.

An alternative method is to carefully study the ingredients in the diet to which your dog is allergic or intolerant. Identify the main ingredient in this diet and eliminate it by buying a different food which does not have that ingredient. Keep experimenting until the symptoms disappear after one month on the new diet.

A male dog flea,
*Ctenocephalides
canis.*

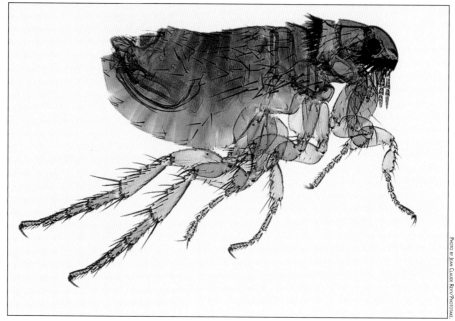

A male dog flea,
*Ctenocephalides
canis.*

EXTERNAL PARASITES

FLEAS

Of all the problems to which dogs are prone, none is more well known and frustrating than fleas. Flea infestation is relatively simple to cure but difficult to prevent. Parasites that are harbored inside the body are a bit more difficult to eradicate but they are easier to control.

To control flea infestation, you have to understand the flea's life cycle. Fleas are often thought of as a summertime problem, but centrally heated homes have changed the patterns and fleas can be found at any time of the year. The most effective method of flea control is a two-stage approach: one stage to kill the adult fleas, and the other to control the development of pre-adult fleas. Unfortunately, no single active ingredient is effective against all stages of the life cycle.

FLEA KILLER CAUTION—"POISON"

Flea-killers are poisonous. You should not spray these toxic chemicals on areas of a dog's body that he licks, including his genitals and his face. Flea killers taken internally are a better answer, but check with your vet in case internal therapy is not advised for your dog.

LIFE CYCLE STAGES

During its life, a flea will pass through four life stages: egg, larva, pupa or nymph and adult. The adult stage is the most visible and irritating stage of the flea life cycle, and this is why the majority of flea-control products concentrate on this stage. The fact is that adult fleas account for only 1% of the total flea population, and the other 99% exist in pre-adult stages, i.e., eggs, larvae and nymphs. The pre-adult stages are barely visible to the naked eye.

THE LIFE CYCLE OF THE FLEA

Eggs are laid on the dog, usually in quantities of about 20 or 30, several times a day. The adult female flea must have a blood meal before each egg-laying session. When first laid, the eggs will cling to the dog's hair, as the eggs are still moist. However, they will quickly dry out and fall from the dog, especially if the dog moves around or scratches. Many eggs will fall off in the dog's favorite area or an area in which he spends a lot of time, such as his bed.

Once the eggs fall from the dog onto the carpet or furniture, they will hatch into larvae. This takes from one to ten days. Larvae are not particularly mobile and will usually travel only a few inches from where they hatch. However, they do have a tendency to move away from bright light and heavy

EN GARDE:
CATCHING FLEAS OFF GUARD!
Consider the following ways to arm yourself against fleas:
- Add a small amount of pennyroyal or eucalyptus oil to your dog's bath. These natural remedies repel fleas.
- Supplement your dog's food with fresh garlic (minced or grated) and a hearty amount of brewer's yeast, both of which ward off fleas.
- Use a flea comb on your dog daily. Submerge fleas in a cup of bleach to kill them quickly.
- Confine the dog to only a few rooms to limit the spread of fleas in the home.
- Vacuum daily...and get all of the crevices! Dispose of the bag every few days until the problem is under control.
- Wash your dog's bedding daily. Cover cushions where your dog sleeps with towels, and wash the towels often.

traffic—under furniture and behind doors are common places to find high quantities of flea larvae.

The flea larvae feed on dead organic matter, including adult flea feces, until they are ready to change into adult fleas. Fleas will usually remain as larvae for around seven days. After this period, the larvae will pupate into protective pupae. While inside the pupae, the larvae will undergo metamorphosis and change into adult fleas. This can take as little time as a few days, but the adult fleas can remain inside the pupae waiting to hatch for up to two years. The pupae are signaled to hatch by certain stimuli, such as physical pressure—the pupae's being stepped on, heat from an animal's lying on the pupae or increased carbon-dioxide levels and vibrations—indicating that a suitable host is available.

Once hatched, the adult flea must feed within a few days. Once the adult flea finds a host, it will not leave voluntarily. It only becomes dislodged by grooming or the host animal's scratching.

The adult flea will remain on the host for the duration of its life unless forcibly removed.

TREATING THE ENVIRONMENT AND THE DOG

Treating fleas should be a two-pronged attack. First, the environment needs to be treated; this includes carpets and furniture, especially the dog's bedding and areas underneath furniture. The environment should be treated with a household spray containing an Insect Growth Regulator (IGR) and an insecticide to kill the adult fleas. Most IGRs are effective against eggs and larvae; they actually mimic the fleas' own hormones and stop the eggs and larvae from developing into adult fleas. There are currently no treatments available to attack the pupa stage of the life cycle, so the adult insecticide is used to kill the newly hatched adult fleas before they find a host. Most IGRs are active for many months, while

A scanning electron micrograph of a dog or cat flea, *Ctenocephalides*, magnified more than 100x. This image has been colorized for effect.

THE LIFE CYCLE OF THE FLEA

Adult

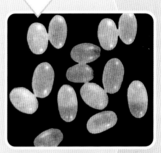

Egg

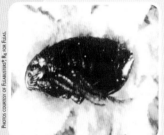

Pupa or Nymph

Larva

PHOTOS COURTESY OF FLEABUSTERS® Rx FOR FLEAS.

Fleas have been around for millions of years and have adapted to changing host animals. They are able to go through a complete life cycle in less than one month or they can extend their lives to almost two years by remaining as pupae or cocoons. They do not need blood or any other food for up to 20 months.

INSECT GROWTH REGULATOR (IGR)

Two types of products should be used when treating fleas—a product to treat the pet and a product to treat the home. Adult fleas represent less than 1% of the flea population. The pre-adult fleas (eggs, larvae and pupae) represent more than 99% of the flea population and are found in the environment; it is in the case of pre-adult fleas that products containing an Insect Growth Regulator (IGR) should be used in the home.

IGRs are a new class of compounds used to prevent the development of insects. They do not kill the insect outright, but instead use the insect's biology against it to stop it from completing its growth. Products that contain methoprene are the world's first and leading IGRs. Used to control fleas and other insects, this type of IGR will stop flea larvae from developing and protect the house for up to seven months.

The American dog tick, *Dermacentor variabilis*, is probably the most common tick found on dogs. Look at the strength in its eight legs! No wonder it's hard to detach them.

The second stage of treatment is to apply an adult insecticide to the dog. Traditionally, this would be in the form of a collar or a spray, but more recent innovations include digestible insecticides that poison the fleas when they ingest the dog's blood. Alternatively, there are drops that, when placed on the back of the dog's neck, spread throughout the hair and skin to kill adult fleas.

Ticks

Though not as common as fleas, ticks are found all over the tropical and temperate world. They don't bite, like fleas; they harpoon. They dig their sharp proboscis (nose) into the dog's

adult insecticides are only active for a few days.

When treating with a house-hold spray, it is a good idea to vacuum before applying the product. This stimulates as many pupae as possible to hatch into adult fleas. The vacuum cleaner should also be treated with an insecticide to prevent the eggs and larvae that have been collected in the vacuum bag from hatching.

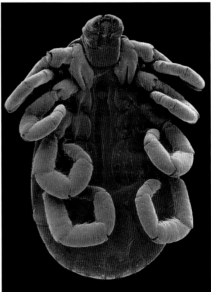

S. E. M. by Dr. Dennis Kunkel, University of Hawaii

skin and drink the blood. Their only food and drink is dog's blood. Dogs can get Lyme disease, Rocky Mountain spotted fever, tick bite paralysis and many other diseases from ticks. They may live where fleas are found and they like to hide in cracks or seams in walls. They are controlled the same way fleas are controlled.

The American dog tick, *Dermacentor variabilis*, may well be the most common dog tick in many geographical areas, especially those areas where the climate is hot and humid. Most dog ticks have life expectancies of a week to six months, depending upon climatic conditions. They can neither jump nor fly, but they can crawl slowly and can range up to 16 feet to reach a sleeping or unsuspecting dog.

MITES

Just as fleas and ticks can be problematic for your dog, mites can also lead to an itchy nuisance. Microscopic in size, mites are related to ticks and generally take up permanent residence on their host animal—in this case, your dog! The term *mange* refers to any infestation caused by one of the mighty mites, of which there are six varieties that concern dog owners.

Demodex mites cause a condition known as demodicosis

DEER-TICK CROSSING

The great outdoors may be fun for your dog, but it also is an home to dangerous ticks. Deer ticks carry a bacterium known as *Borrelia burgdorferi* and are most active in the autumn and spring. When infections are caught early, penicillin and tetracycline are effective antibiotics, but if left untreated the bacteria may cause neurological, kidney and cardiac problems as well as long-term trouble with walking and painful joints.

S. E. M. BY DR. ANDREW SPIELMAN/PHOTOTAKE.

PHOTO BY DR. DENNIS KUNKEL, UNIVERSITY OF HAWAII.

The head of an American dog tick, *Dermacentor variabilis*, enlarged and colorized for effect.

The mange mite, *Psoroptes bovis*, can infest cattle and other domestic animals.

PHOTO BY JAMES HAYDEN/YOAV/PHOTOTAKE

(sometimes called red mange or follicular mange), in which the mites live in the dog's hair follicles and sebaceous glands. This type of mange is commonly passed from the dam to her puppies and usually shows up on the puppies' muzzles, though demodicosis is not transferable from one normal dog to another. Most dogs recover from this type of mange without any treatment, though topical therapies are commonly prescribed by the vet.

Human lice look like dog lice; the two are closely related.

PHOTO BY DWIGHT R. KUHN.

The *Cheyletiellosis* mite is the hook-mouthed culprit associated with "walking dandruff," a condition that affects dogs as well as cats and rabbits. This mite lives on the surface of the animal's skin and is readily transferable through direct or indirect contact with an affected animal. The dandruff is present in the form of scaly skin, which may or may not be itchy. If not treated, this mange can affect a whole kennel of dogs and can be spread to humans as well.

The *Sarcoptes* mite causes intense itching on the dog in the form of a condition known as scabies or sarcoptic mange. The cycle of the *Sarcoptes* mite lasts about three weeks, and the mites live in the top layer of the dog's skin (epidermis), preferably in areas with little hair. Scabies is highly contagious and can be passed to humans. Sometimes an allergic reaction to the mite worsens the severe itching associated with sarcoptic mange.

Ear mites, *Otodectes cynotis,* lead to otodectic mange, which most commonly affects the outer ear canal of the dog, though other areas can be affected as well. Dogs with ear-mite infestation commonly scratch at their ears, causing further irritation, and shake their heads. Dark brown droppings in the outer ear confirm the diagnosis. Your vet can prescribe a treatment to flush out the ears and kill any eggs in the ears. A complete month of treatment is necessary to cure the mange.

Two other mites, less common in dogs, include *Dermanyssus gallinae* (the poultry or red mite) and *Eutrombicula alfreddugesi* (the North American mite associated with trombiculidiasis or chigger infestation). The poultry mite frequently lives on chickens, but can transfer to dogs who spend time near farm animals. Chigger

DO NOT MIX
Never mix pest control products without first consulting your vet. Some products can become toxic when combined with others and can cause fatal consequences.

NOT A DROP TO DRINK
Never allow your dog to swim in polluted water or public areas where water quality can be suspect. Even perfectly clear water can harbor parasites, many of which can cause serious to fatal illnesses in canines. Areas inhabited by water-fowl and other wildlife are especially dangerous.

infestation affects dogs in the Central U.S. who have exposure to woodlands. The types of mange caused by both of these mites are treatable by veterinarians.

INTERNAL PARASITES
Most animals—fishes, birds and mammals, including dogs and humans—have worms and other parasites that live inside their bodies. According to Dr. Herbert R. Axelrod, the fish pathologist, there are two kinds of parasites: dumb and smart. The smart parasites live in peaceful cooperation with their hosts (symbiosis), while the dumb parasites kill their hosts. Most worm infections are relatively easy to control. If they are not controlled, they weaken the host dog to the point that other medical problems occur, but they do not kill the host as dumb parasites would.

A brown dog tick, *Rhipicephalus sanguineus,* **is an uncommon but annoying tick found on dogs.** Photo by Carolina Biological Supply/Phototake.

Photo by Carolina Biological Supply/PhotoTake

The roundworm *Rhabditis* can infect both dogs and humans.

The roundworm, *Ascaris lumbricoides.*

ROUNDWORMS

Average-size dogs can pass 1,360,000 roundworm eggs every day. For example, if there were only 1 million dogs in the world, the world would be saturated with thousands of tons of dog feces. These feces would contain around 15,000,000,000 roundworm eggs.

Up to 31% of home yards and children's sand boxes in the US contain roundworm eggs.

Flushing dog's feces down the toilet is not a safe practice because the usual sewage treatments do not destroy roundworm eggs.

Infected puppies start shedding roundworm eggs at three weeks of age. They can be infected by their mother's milk.

ROUNDWORMS

The roundworms that infect dogs are known scientifically as *Toxocara canis*. They live in the dog's intestines and shed eggs continually. It has been estimated that a dog produces about 6 or more ounces of feces every day. Each ounce of feces averages hundreds of thousands of roundworm eggs. There are no known areas in which dogs roam that do not contain roundworm eggs. The greatest danger of roundworms is that they infect people, too! It is wise to have your dog tested regularly for roundworms.

In young puppies, roundworms cause bloated bellies, diarrhea, coughing and vomiting, and are transmitted from the dam (through blood or milk). Affected puppies will not appear as animated as normal puppies. The worms appear spaghetti-like, measuring as long as 6 inches. Adult dogs can acquire roundworms through coprophagia (eating contaminated feces) or by killing rodents that carry roundworms.

Roundworm infection can kill puppies and cause severe problems in adults, as the hatched larvae travel to the lungs and trachea through the bloodstream. Cleanliness is the best preventative for roundworms. Always pick up after your dog and dispose of feces in appropriate receptacles.

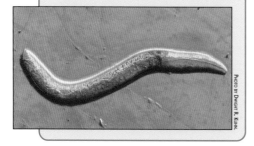

Photo by Dwight R. Kuhn.

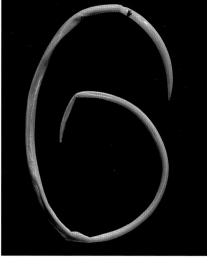

Photo by Dwight R. Kuhn.

HOOKWORMS

In the United States, dog owners have to be concerned about four different species of hookworm, the most common and most serious of which is *Ancylostoma caninum,* which prefers warm climates. The others are *Ancylostoma braziliense, Ancylostoma tubaeforme* and *Uncinaria stenocephala,* the latter of which is a concern to dogs living in the Northern U.S. and Canada, as this species prefers cold climates. Hookworms are dangerous to humans as well as to dogs and cats, and can be the cause of severe anemia due to iron deficiency. The worm uses its teeth to attach itself to the dog's intestines and changes the site of its attachment about six times per day. Each time the worm repositions itself, the dog loses

blood and can become anemic. *Ancylostoma caninum* is the most likely of the four species to cause anemia in the dog.

Symptoms of hookworm infection include dark stools, weight loss, general weakness, pale coloration and anemia, as well as possible skin problems. Fortunately, hookworms are easily purged from the affected dog with a number of medications that have proven effective. Discuss these with your veterinarian. Most heartworm preventatives include a hookworm insecticide as well.

Owners also must be aware that hookworms can infect humans, who can acquire the larvae through exposure to contaminated feces. Since the worms cannot complete their life cycle on a human, the worms simply infest the skin and cause irritation. This condition is known as cutaneous larva migrans syndrome. As a preventative, use disposable gloves or a "poop-scoop" to pick up your dog's droppings and prevent your dog (or neighborhood cats) from defecating in children's play areas.

The hookworm, *Ancylostoma caninum.*

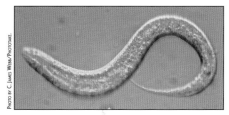

Photo by C. James Webb/Phototake.

The infective stage of the hookworm larva.

TAPEWORMS

Humans, rats, squirrels, foxes, coyotes, wolves and domestic dogs are all susceptible to tapeworm infection. Except in humans, tapeworms are usually not a fatal infection. Infected individuals can harbor 1000 parasitic worms.

Tapeworms, like some other types of worm, are hermaphroditic, meaning male and female in the same worm.

If dogs eat infected rats or mice, or anything else infected with tapeworm, they get the tapeworm disease. One month after attaching to a dog's intestine, the worm starts shedding eggs. These eggs are infective immediately. Infective eggs can live for a few months without a host animal.

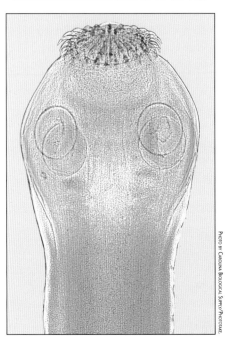

The head and rostellum (the round prominence on the scolex) of a tapeworm, which infects dogs and humans.

PHOTO BY CAROLINA BIOLOGICAL SUPPLY/PHOTOTAKE.

TAPEWORMS

There are many species of tapeworm, all of which are carried by fleas! The most common tapeworm affecting dogs is known as *Dipylidium caninum*. The dog eats the flea and starts the tapeworm cycle. Humans can also be infected with tapeworms—so don't eat fleas! Fleas are so small that your dog could pass them onto your hands, your plate or your food and thus make it possible for you to ingest a flea that is carrying tapeworm eggs.

While tapeworm infection is not life-threatening in dogs (smart parasite!), it can be the cause of a very serious liver disease for humans. About 50% of the humans infected with *Echinococcus multilocularis*, a type of tapeworm that causes alveolar hydatid, perish.

WHIPWORMS

In North America, whipworms are counted among the most common parasitic worms in dogs. The whipworm's scientific name is *Trichuris vulpis*. These worms attach themselves in the lower parts of the intestine, where they feed. Affected dogs may only experience upset tummies, colic and diarrhea. These worms, however, can live for months or years in the dog, beginning their larval stage in the small intestine, spending their adult stage in the large intestine and finally passing infective eggs through the dog's feces. The only way to detect whipworms is through a fecal examination, though this is not always foolproof. Treatment for whipworms is tricky, due to the worms' unusual life-cycle pattern, and very often dogs are reinfected due to exposure to infective eggs on the ground. The whipworm eggs can survive in the environment for as long as five years, thus cleaning up droppings in your own backyard as well as in public places is absolutely essential for sanitation purposes and the health of your dog and others.

THREADWORMS

Though less common than round-worms, hookworms and those previously mentioned, thread-worms concern dog owners in the Southwestern U.S. and Gulf Coast area where the climate is hot and humid. Living in the small intestine of the dog, this worm measures a mere 2 millimeters and is round in shape. Like that of the whip-worm, the threadworm's life cycle is very complex and the eggs and larvae are passed through the feces. A deadly disease in humans, *Strongyloides* readily infects people, and the handling of feces is the most common means of transmission. Threadworms are most often seen in young puppies; bloody diarrhea and pneumonia are symptoms. Sick puppies must be isolated and treated immediately; vets recommend a follow-up treatment one month later.

HEARTWORM PREVENTATIVES

There are many heartworm preventatives on the market, many of which are sold at your veterinarian's office. These products can be given daily or monthly, depending on the manufacturer's instructions. All of these preventatives contain chemical insecticides directed at killing heartworms, which leads to some controversy among dog owners. In effect, heartworm preventatives are necessary evils, though you should determine how necessary based on your pet's lifestyle. There is no doubt that heartworm is a dreadful disease that threatens the life of dogs. However, the likelihood of your dog's being bitten by an infected mosquito is slim in most places, and a mosquito-repellent (or an herbal remedy such as Wormwood or

Black Walnut) is much safer for your dog and will not compromise his immune system (the way heartworm preventatives will). Should you decide to use the traditional preventative "medications," you can consider giving the pill every other or third month. Since the toxins in the pill will kill the heartworms at all stages of development, the pill would be effective in killing larvae, nymphs or adults and it takes four months for the larvae to reach the adult stage. Thus, there is no rationale to poisoning the dog's system on a monthly basis. Lastly, do not give the pill during the winter months since there are no mosquitoes around to pass on their infection, unless you live in a tropical environment.

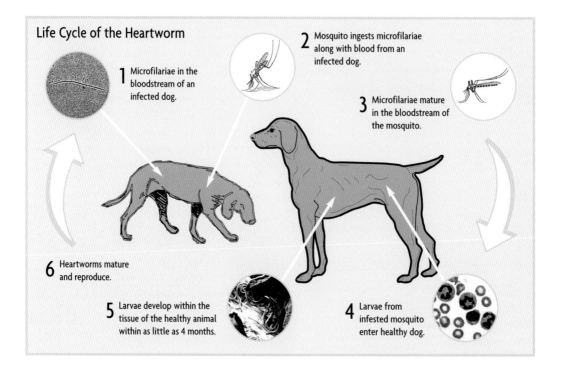

Life Cycle of the Heartworm

1 Microfilariae in the bloodstream of an infected dog.

2 Mosquito ingests microfilariae along with blood from an infected dog.

3 Microfilariae mature in the bloodstream of the mosquito.

6 Heartworms mature and reproduce.

5 Larvae develop within the tissue of the healthy animal within as little as 4 months.

4 Larvae from infested mosquito enter healthy dog.

HEARTWORMS

Heartworms are thin, extended worms up to 12 inches long, which live in a dog's heart and the major blood vessels surrounding it. Dogs may have up to 200 worms. Symptoms may be loss of energy, loss of appetite, coughing, the development of a pot belly and anemia.

Heartworms are transmitted by mosquitoes. The mosquito drinks the blood of an infected dog and takes in larvae with the blood. The larvae, called microfilariae, develop within the body of the mosquito and are passed on to the next dog bitten after the larvae mature. It takes two to three weeks for the larvae to develop to the infective stage within the body of the mosquito. Dogs are usually treated at about six weeks of age and maintained on a prophylactic dose given monthly.

Blood testing for heartworms is not necessarily indicative of how seriously your dog is infected. Although this is a dangerous disease, it is not easy for a dog to be infected. Discuss the various preventatives with your vet, as there are many different types now available. Together you can decide on a safe course of prevention for your dog.

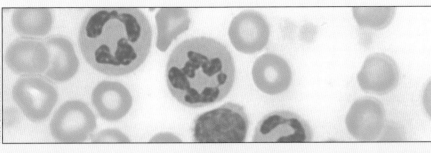

Photo by Carolina Biological Supply/Phototake.

Magnified heart-
worm larvae,
Dirofilaria immitis.

Heartworm,
*Dirofilaria
immitis.*

Photo by J E Hayden, RBP/Phototake.

The heart
of a dog infected
with canine heart-
worm, *Dirofilaria
immitis.*

Photo by James E. Hayden, RPB/Phototake.

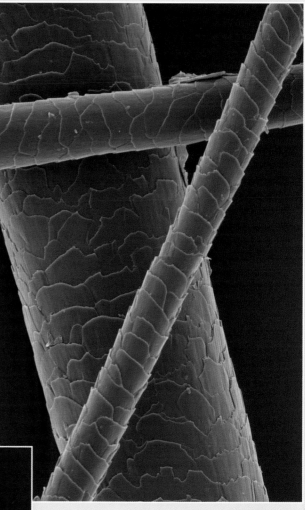

Rottweiler hairs greatly magnified. The S.E.M. above shows top coat and undercoat hairs in good condition. The S.E.M. below left shows a hair in poor condition, as evidenced by the lack of uniformity of the cuticle. The S.E.M. above left shows split ends. S.E.M. by Dr. Dennis Kunkel, University of Hawaii.

First Aid at a Glance

Burns
Place the affected area under cool water; use ice if only a small area is burnt.

Bee Stings/Insect bites
Apply ice to relieve swelling; antihistamine dosed properly.

Animal bites
Clean any bleeding area; apply pressure until bleeding subsides; go to the vet.

Spider bites
Use cold compress and a pressurized pack to inhibit venom's spreading.

Antifreeze poisoning
Induce vomiting with hydrogen peroxide. Seek *immediate* veterinary help!

Fish hooks
Removal best handled by vet; hook must be cut in order to remove.

Snake bites
Pack ice around bite; contact vet quickly; identify snake for proper antivenin.

Car accident
Move dog from roadway with blanket; seek veterinary aid.

Shock
Calm the dog, keep him warm; seek immediate veterinary help.

Nosebleed
Apply cold compress to the nose; apply pressure to any visible abrasion.

Bleeding
Apply pressure above the area; treat wound by applying a cotton pack.

Heat stroke
Submerge dog in cold bath; cool down with fresh air and water; go to the vet.

Frostbite/Hypothermia
Warm the dog with a warm bath, electric blankets or hot water bottles.

Abrasions
Clean the wound and wash out thoroughly with fresh water; apply antiseptic.

!! *Remember: an injured dog may attempt to bite a helping hand from fear and confusion. Always muzzle the dog before trying to offer assistance.* **!!**

When your Rottweiler starts to slow down, rest a lot and stop running to greet you, you know he is getting old.

Your Senior Rottweiler

The term *old* is a qualitative term. For dogs, as well as for their masters, *old* is relative. Certainly we can all distinguish between a puppy Rottie and an adult Rottie—there are the obvious physical traits, such as size, appearance and facial expressions, and personality traits. Puppies and young dogs like to play with children. Children's natural exuberance is a good match for the seemingly endless energy of young dogs. They like to run, jump, chase and retrieve. When dogs grow older and cease their interaction with children, they are often thought of as being too old to keep up with the kids. On the other hand, if a Rottweiler is only exposed to people with quieter lifestyles, his life will normally be less active and the decrease in his activity level as he ages will not be as obvious.

If people live to be 100 years old, dogs live to be 20 years old. While this might seem like a good rule of thumb, it is very inaccurate. When trying to compare dog years to human years, you cannot make a gener-

When the Rottweiler gets old, he will prefer to sit and await your arrival instead of jumping with joy in the way he may previously have responded.

alization about all dogs. While most large-breed dogs do not last until ten years of age, the Rottie commonly does! Dogs generally are considered physically mature at three years of age (or earlier), but can reproduce even earlier. The Rottweiler is not considered physically mature, in some cases, until two to three years of age. Generally speaking, the first three years of a dog's life are like seven times that of comparable humans. That means a 3-year-old dog is like a 21-year-old human. As the curve of comparison shows, however, there is no hard and fast rule for comparing dog and human ages. Small breeds tend to live longer than large

SENIOR SIGNS

An old dog starts to show one or more of the following symptoms:

- The hair on the face and paws starts to turn gray. The color breakdown usually starts around the eyes and mouth.
- Sleep patterns are deeper and longer, and the old dog is harder to awaken.
- Food intake diminishes.
- Responses to calls, whistles and other signals are ignored more and more.
- Eye contact does not evoke tail wagging (assuming it once did).

breeds, some breeds' adolescent periods last longer than others' and some breeds experience rapid periods of growth. The comparison is made even more difficult, for, likewise, not all humans age at the same rate...and human females live longer than human males.

WHAT TO LOOK FOR IN SENIORS

Most vets and behaviorists use the seven-year-old mark as the time to consider a dog a senior, though some breeders prefer to wait until the Rottweiler is eight

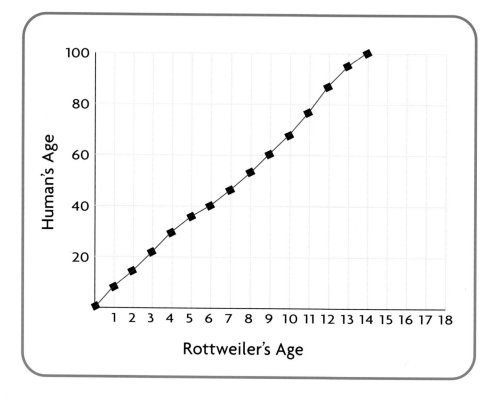

or nine years of age. Nevertheless, the term "senior" does not imply that the dog is geriatric and has begun to fail in mind and body. Aging is essentially a slowing process. Humans readily admit that they feel a difference in their activity level from age 20 to 30, and then from 30 to 40, etc. By treating the seven-year-old dog as a senior, owners are able to implement certain therapeutic and preventative medical strategies with the help of their veterinarians. A senior-care program should include at least two veterinary visits per year and screening sessions to determine the dog's health status, as well as nutritional counseling. Vets determine the senior dog's health status through a blood smear for a complete blood count, serum chemistry profile with electrolytes, urinalysis, blood pressure check, electrocardiogram, ocular tonometry (pressure on the eyeball) and dental prophylaxis.

Such an extensive program for senior dogs is well advised before owners start to see the obvious physical signs of aging, such as slower and inhibited movement, graying, increased sleep/nap periods and disinterest in play and other activity. This preventative program promises a longer, healthier life for the aging dog. Among the physical problems common in aging dogs are the loss of sight and hearing, arthritis, kidney and liver failure, diabetes mellitus, heart disease and Cushing's disease (a hormonal disease).

In addition to the physical manifestations discussed, there are some behavioral changes and problems related to aging dogs. Dogs suffering from hearing or vision loss, dental discomfort or arthritis can become aggressive. Likewise, the near-deaf and/or blind dog may be startled more easily and react in an unexpect-

---

NOTICING THE SYMPTOMS

The symptoms listed below are symptoms that gradually appear and become more noticeable. They are not life-threatening; however, the symptoms below are to be taken very seriously and warrant a discussion with your veterinarian:

- Your dog cries and whimpers when he moves, and he stops running completely.
- Convulsions start or become more serious and frequent. The usual convulsion (spasm) is when the dog stiffens and starts to tremble, being unable or unwilling to move. The seizure usually lasts for 5 to 30 minutes.
- Your dog drinks more water and urinates more frequently. Wetting and bowel accidents take place indoors without warning.
- Vomiting becomes more and more frequent.

edly aggressive manner. Seniors suffering from senility can become more impatient and irritable. Housesoiling accidents are associated with loss of mobility, kidney problems and loss of sphincter control as well as plaque accumulation, physiological brain changes and reactions to medications. Older dogs, just like young puppies, suffer from separation anxiety, which can lead to excessive barking, whining, housesoiling and destructive behavior. Seniors may become fearful of everyday sounds, such as vacuum cleaners, heaters, thunder and passing traffic. Some dogs have difficulty sleeping, due to discomfort, the need for frequent relief and the like.

Owners should avoid spoiling the older dog with too many treats. Obesity is a common problem in older dogs and subtracts years from their

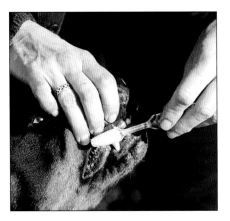

As your Rottweiler gets older, pay more attention during his routine dental care to check for tooth decay and gum disease.

lives. Keep the senior dog as trim as possible, since excess weight puts additional stress on the body's vital organs. Some breeders recommend supplementing the diet with foods high in fiber and lower in calories. Adding fresh vegetables and marrow broth to the senior's diet makes a tasty, low-calorie, low-fat supplement. Vets also offer specialty diets for senior dogs that are worth exploring.

Your dog, as he nears his twilight years, needs your patience and good care more than ever. Never punish an older dog for an accident or abnormal behavior. For all the years of love, protection and companionship that your dog has provided, he deserves special attention and courtesies. The older dog may need to relieve himself at 3 a.m. because he can no longer hold it for eight hours. Older dogs may not be able to remain crated for more than two or three hours. It may be time to give up a sofa or chair to your old friend. Although he may not seem as enthusiastic about your attention and petting, he does appreciate the considerations you offer as he gets older.

Your Rottweiler does not understand why his world is slowing down. Owners must make their dogs' transition into their golden years as pleasant and rewarding as possible.

WHAT TO DO
WHEN THE TIME COMES

You are never fully prepared to make a rational decision about putting your dog to sleep. It is very obvious that you love your Rottweiler or you would not be reading this book. Putting a beloved dog to sleep is extremely difficult. It is a decision that must be made with your vet. You are usually forced to make the decision when your dog experiences one or more life-threatening symptoms that have become serious enough for you to seek veterinary help.

If the prognosis of the malady indicates that the end is near and that your beloved pet will only continue to suffer and experience no enjoyment for the balance of his life, then euthanasia is the right choice.

WHAT IS EUTHANASIA?

Euthanasia derives from the Greek, meaning good death. In other words, it means the planned, painless killing of a dog suffering from a painful, incurable condition, or who is so aged that he cannot walk, see, eat or control his excretory functions. Euthanasia is usually accomplished by injection with an overdose of anesthesia or a barbiturate. Aside from the prick of the needle, the experience is usually painless.

Some pet cemeteries have sites in which you can store your deceased Rottweiler's ashes.

MAKING THE DECISION

The decision to euthanize your dog is never easy. The days during which the dog becomes ill and the end occurs can be unusually stressful for you. If this is your first experience with the death of a loved one, you may need the comfort dictated by your religious beliefs. If you are the head of the family and have children, you should have involved them in the decision of putting your Rottweiler to sleep. Usually your dog can be maintained on drugs for a few days in order to give you ample time to make a decision. During this time, talking with members of your family or with people who have lived through the same experience can ease the burden of your inevitable decision.

THE FINAL RESTING PLACE

Dogs can have some of the same privileges as humans. The remains of your beloved dog can be buried in a pet cemetery, which is generally expensive.

Alternatively, if your dog has died at home, he can be buried in your yard in a spot marked with a stone, flowers or a newly planted tree or shrub. Cremation is also an option; your dog can be cremated individually and the ashes returned to you. A less expensive option is mass cremation, although, of course, the ashes cannot then be returned. Vets can usually help you locate a pet cemetery or arrange the cremation on your behalf. The cost of these options should always be discussed frankly and openly with your vet.

GETTING ANOTHER DOG?

The grief of losing your beloved dog will be as lasting as the grief of losing a human friend or relative. In most cases, if your dog died of old age (if there is such a thing), he had slowed down considerably. Do you want a new Rottweiler puppy to replace him? Or are you better off finding a more mature Rottie, say two to three years of age, which will usually be housebroken and will have an already developed personality. In this case, you can find out if you like each other after a few hours of being together.

The decision is, of course, your own. Do you want another Rottweiler or perhaps a different breed so as to avoid comparison with your beloved friend? Most people usually buy the same breed because they know (and love) the characteristics of that breed. Then, too, they often know people who have the same breed and perhaps they are lucky enough that a breeder whom they know and respect expects a litter soon. What could be better?

Consult your vet to help you locate a pet cemetery in your area.

Showing Your Rottweiler

When you purchase your Rottweiler, you will make it clear to the breeder whether you want one just as a lovable companion and pet, or if you hope to be buying a Rottweiler with show prospects. No reputable breeder will sell you a young puppy and tell you that he is definitely of show quality, for so much can go wrong during the early months of a puppy's development. If you plan to show, what you will hopefully have acquired is a puppy with "show potential."

To the novice, exhibiting a Rottweiler in the show ring may look easy, but it takes a lot of hard work and devotion to do top winning at a show such as the prestigious Westminster Kennel Club dog show, not to mention a little luck too!

The first concept that the canine novice learns when watching a dog show is that each dog first competes against members of his own breed. Once the judge has selected the best member of each breed (Best of Breed), provided that the show is judged on a Group system, that chosen dog will compete with other Best of Breed dogs in his group. Finally, the dogs chosen first in each group will compete for the top award, Best in Show.

The second concept that you must understand is that the dogs are not actually compared against one another. The judge compares each dog against his breed standard, the approved word depiction of the ideal specimen that is approved by the American Kennel Club (AKC). While some early breed standards were indeed based on specific dogs that were famous or popular, many dedicated enthusiasts say that a perfect specimen, as described in the standard, has never walked into a show ring, has never been bred and, to the woe of dog breeders around the globe, does not exist. Breeders attempt to get as close to this ideal as possible with every litter, but theoretically the "perfect" dog is so elusive that it is impossible. (And if the "perfect" dog were born, breeders and judges would never agree that it was indeed "perfect.")

If you are interested in exploring the world of dog showing, your best bet is to join your local breed club or the national club, which is the American Rottweiler Club, or one of the other large breed clubs. These clubs often host both regional and national specialties, shows only for Rottweilers, which can include conformation as well as obedience, tracking, herding and agility trials. Even if you have no intention of competing with your Rottweiler, a specialty is like a festival for lovers of the breed who congregate to share their favorite topic: Rottweilers! Clubs also send out newsletters, and some organize training days and seminars in order that people may learn more about their chosen breed. To locate the breed club closest to you, contact the American Kennel Club, which furnishes the rules and regulations for all of these events plus general dog registration and other basic requirements of dog ownership.

The American Kennel Club offers three kinds of conformation shows: an all-breed show (for all AKC-recognized breeds), a specialty show (for one breed only, usually sponsored by the parent club) and a Group show (for all breeds in the Group).

For a dog to become an AKC champion of record, the dog must accumulate 15 points at the shows from at least three different judges, including two "majors." A "major" is defined as a three-, four- or five-point win, and the number of points per win is determined by the number of dogs entered in the show on the day. Depending on the breed, the number of points that are awarded varies. In a breed as popular as the Rottweiler, more dogs are needed to rack up the points. At any dog show, only one dog and one bitch of each breed can win points.

Dog showing does not offer "co-ed" classes. Dogs and bitches never compete against each other in the classes. Non-champion dogs are called "class dogs" because they compete in one of five classes. A dog is entered in a particular class depending on his age and previous show wins. To begin, there is the Puppy Class (for 6- to 9-month-olds and for 9- to 12-month-olds); this class is followed by the Novice Class (for dogs that have not won any first prizes except in the Puppy Class or three first prizes in the Novice Class and have not accumulated any points toward their champion title); the Bred-by-Exhibitor Class (for dogs handled by their breeders or handled by one of the breeder's immediate family); the American-bred Class (for dogs bred in the USA!); and the Open Class (for any dog that is not a champion).

Dog showing is fun and educational, and it can also be very rewarding.

The judge at the show begins judging the Puppy Class, first dogs and then bitches, and proceeds through the classes. The judge places his winners first through fourth in each class. In the Winners Class, the first-place winners of each class compete with one another to determine Winners Dog and Winners Bitch. The judge also places a Reserve Winners Dog and Reserve Winners Bitch, which could be awarded the points in the case of a disqualification. The Winners Dog and Winners Bitch, the two that are awarded the points for the breed, then compete with any champions of record entered in the show. The judge reviews the Winners Dog, Winners Bitch and all of the champions to select his Best of Breed. The Best of Winners is selected between the Winners Dog and Winners Bitch. Were one of these two to be selected Best of Breed, this dog would automatically be named Best of Winners as well. Finally the judge selects his Best of Opposite Sex to the Best of Breed winner.

At a Group show or all-breed show, the Best of Breed winners from each breed then compete against one another for Group One through Group Four. The judge compares each Best of Breed to his breed standard, and the dog that most closely lives up to the ideal for his breed is selected as Group One. Finally, all seven group

winners (from the Working Group, Sporting Group, Hound Group, etc.) compete for Best in Show.

To find out about dog shows in your area, you can subscribe to the American Kennel Club's monthly magazine, The *American Kennel Gazette* and the accompanying *Events Calendar*. You can also look in your local newspaper for advertisements for dog shows in your area or go on the Internet to the AKC's website, www.akc.org.

If your Rottweiler is six months of age or older and registered with the AKC, you can enter him in a dog show where the breed is offered classes. Provided that your Rottweiler does not have a disqualifying fault, he can compete. Only unaltered dogs can be entered in a dog show, so if you have spayed or neutered your Rottweiler, you cannot compete in conformation shows. The reason for this is simple. Dog shows are the main forum to prove which representatives in a breed are

You don't have to be an expert to get started in showing your Rottweiler. Every handler was a beginner at one time.

worthy of being bred. Only dogs that have achieved championships—the AKC "seal of approval" for quality in pure-bred dogs—should be bred. Altered dogs, however, can participate in other AKC events such as obedience trials and the Canine Good Citizen program.

Before you actually step into the ring, you would be well advised to sit back and observe the judge's ring procedure. If it is your first time in the ring, do not be over-anxious and run to the front of the line. It is much better to stand back and study how the exhibitor in front of you is performing. The judge asks each handler to "stack" the dog, hopefully showing the dog off to his best advantage. The judge will observe the dog from a distance and from different angles, and approach the dog to check his teeth, overall structure, alertness and muscle tone, as well as consider how well the dog "conforms" to the standard. Most importantly, the judge will have the exhibitor move the dog around the ring in some pattern that he should specify (another advantage to not going first, but always listen since some judges change their directions—and the judge is always right!). Finally, the judge will give the dog one last look before moving on to the next exhibitor.

If you are not in the top four in your class at your first show, do

> ## SHOW-RING ETIQUETTE
> Just as with anything else, there is a certain etiquette to the show ring that can only be learned through experience. Showing your dog can be quite intimidating to you as a novice when it seems as if everyone else knows what he is doing. You can familiarize yourself with ring procedure beforehand by taking showing classes to prepare you and your dog for conformation showing and by talking with experienced handlers. When you are in the ring, it is very important to pay attention and listen to the instructions you are given by the judge about where to move your dog. Remember, even the most skilled handlers had to start somewhere. Keep it up and you too will become a proficient handler as you gain practice and experience.

not be discouraged. Be patient and consistent, and you may eventually find yourself in a winning line-up. Remember that the winners were once in your shoes and have devoted many hours and much money to earn the placement. If you find that your dog is losing every time and never getting a nod, it may be time to consider a different dog sport or to just enjoy your Rottweiler as a pet. Parent clubs offer other events, such as agility, tracking, obedience, herding, instinct tests and more, which may be of interest to the owner of a well-trained Rottweiler.

OBEDIENCE TRIALS

Obedience trials in the U.S. trace back to the early 1930s when organized obedience training was developed to demonstrate how well dog and owner could work together. The pioneer of obedience trials is Mrs. Helen Whitehouse Walker, a Standard Poodle fancier, who designed a series of exercises after the Associated Sheep, Police Army Dog Society of Great Britain. Since the early days, obedience trials have grown by leaps and bounds, and today there are over 2,000 trials held in the U.S. every year, with more than 100,000 dogs competing. Any AKC-registered dog can enter an obedience trial, regardless of conformational disqualifications or neutering.

Obedience trials are divided into three levels of progressive difficulty. At the first level, the Novice, dogs compete for the title Companion Dog (CD); at the intermediate level, the Open, dogs compete for the title Companion Dog Excellent (CDX); and at the advanced level, dogs compete for the title Utility Dog (UD). Classes are sub-divided into "A" (for beginners) and "B" (for more experienced handlers). A perfect score at any level is 200, and a dog must score 170 or better to earn a "leg," of which three are needed to earn the title. To earn points, the dog must score more than 50% of the available points in each exercise; the possible points range from 20 to 40.

Each level consists of a different set of exercises. In the Novice level, the dog must heel on and off lead, come, long sit, long down and stand for examination. These skills are the basic ones required for a well-behaved "Companion Dog." The Open level requires that the dog perform the same exercises above but without a leash for extended lengths of time, as well as retrieve a dumbbell, broad jump and drop on recall. In the Utility level, dogs must perform ten difficult exercises, including scent discrimination, hand signals for basic commands, directed jump and directed retrieve.

Once a dog has earned the UD title, he can compete with other proven obedience dogs for the coveted title of Utility Dog Excellent

An aspiring show dog starts training for the ring at an early age.

Champion Rottweilers do not necessarily make better pets than those that are not show quality...but what a joy when you can have both a great pet and a champion in the same dog!

Rottweilers can easily be trained for agility trials. It's fun for both dog and handler!

(UDX), which requires that the dog win "legs" in ten shows. Utility Dogs who earn "legs" in Open B and Utility B earn points toward their Obedience Trial Champion title. In 1977, the title Obedience Trial Champion (OTCh.) was established by the AKC. To become an OTCh., a dog needs to earn 100 points, which requires three first places in Open B and Utility under three different judges.

The Grand Prix of obedience trials, the AKC National Obedience Invitational gives qualifying Utility Dogs the chance to win the newest and highest title: National Obedience Champion (NOC). Only the top 25 ranked obedience dogs, plus any dog ranked in the top 3 in his breed, are allowed to compete.

TRACKING

Any dog is capable of tracking, using his nose to follow a trail. Tracking tests are exciting and

At first you will have to manipulate your Rottweiler into the standing position, but after he is used to it he should assume the position on your command.

competitive ways to test your Rottweiler's ability to search and rescue. The AKC started tracking tests in 1937, when the first AKC-licensed test took place as part of the Utility level at an obedience trial. Ten years later in 1947, the AKC offered the first title, Tracking Dog (TD). It was not until 1980 that the AKC added the Tracking Dog Excellent title (TDX), which was followed by the Versatile Surface Tracking title (VST) in 1995. The title Champion Tracker (CT) is awarded to a dog who has earned all three titles.

In the beginning level of tracking, the owner follows the dog through a field on a long lead. To earn the TD title, the dog must follow a track laid by a human 30 to 120 minutes prior. The track is about 500 yards long with up to five directional changes. The TDX requires that the dog follow a track that is three to five hours old over a course up to 1,000 yards long

Practice with your Rottweiler as much as possible to be sure he becomes accustomed to standing politely.

with up to seven directional changes. The VST requires that the dog follow a track up to five hours old through an urban setting.

AGILITY TRIALS

Having had its origins in the U.K. back in 1977, AKC agility had its official beginning in the U.S. in August 1994, when the first licensed agility trials were held. The AKC allows all registered breeds (including Miscellaneous Class breeds) to participate, providing the dog is 12 months of age or older. Agility is designed so that the handler demonstrates how well the dog can work at his side. The handler directs his dog over an obstacle course that includes jumps as well as tires, the dog walk, weave poles, pipe tunnels, collapsed tunnels, etc. While working his way through the course, the dog must keep one eye and ear on the handler and the rest

Rottweilers at a dog show awaiting their turn in the ring.

INFORMATION ON CLUBS

You can get information about dog shows from the national kennel clubs:

American Kennel Club
5580 Centerview Dr., Raleigh, NC 27606-3390
www.akc.org

United Kennel Club
100 E. Kilgore Road, Kalamazoo, MI 49002
www.ukcdogs.com

Canadian Kennel Club
89 Skyway Ave., Suite 100, Etobicoke, Ontario
M9W 6R4 Canada
www.ckc.ca

The Kennel Club
1-5 Clarges St., Piccadilly, London W1Y 8AB, UK
www.the-kennel-club.org.uk

---

of his body on the course. The handler gives verbal and hand signals to guide the dog through the course.

The first organization to promote agility trials in the U.S. was the United States Dog Agility Association, Inc. (USDAA), which was established in 1986 and spawned numerous member clubs around the country. Both the USDAA and the AKC offers titles to winning dogs. Three titles are available through the USDAA: Agility Dog (AD), Advanced Agility Dog (AAD) and Master Agility Dog (MAD). The AKC offers Novice Agility (NA), Open Agility (OA), Agility Excellent (AX) and Master Agility Excellent (MX). Beyond these four AKC titles, dogs can win additional ones in "jumper" classes, Jumpers with Weave Novice (NAJ), Open (OAJ) and Excellent (MXJ), which lead to the ultimate title(s): MACH, Master Agility Champion. Dogs can continue to add number designations to the MACH titles, indicating how many times the dog has met the MACH requirements, such as MACH1, MACH2, etc.

Agility is great fun for dog and owner with many rewards for everyone involved. Interested owners should join a training club that has obstacles and experienced agility handlers who can introduce you and your dog to the "ropes" (and tires, tunnels, etc.).

HERDING TESTS AND TRIALS

Since the first sheepdog trials recorded in the late 19th century in Wales, the practice of herding trials has grown tremendously around the world. The first trial began as a friendly match to see which farmer's dog was the best at moving sheep. Today the sport is more organized than in those early days, and all Herding breeds as well as the Rottie and a few others can earn titles at these fun and competitive events.

The AKC offers herding trials and tests to any eligible dog that is nine months of age or older. The handler is expected to direct the Rottweiler to herd various livestock, including sheep, ducks, goats and cattle. There are two

Winning! How sweet it is!

titles for Herding Tests, Herding Tested (HT) and Pre-Trial Tested (PT). If the dog shows a basic innate ability, he is awarded the HT title; the PT title is awarded to a dog that can herd a small herd of livestock through a basic course.

In herding trials, there are four titles awarded: Herding Started (HS), Herding Intermediate (HI), Herding Excellent (HX) and Herding Champion (HCh.), the latter of which is awarded to a dog who has demonstrated mastery of herding in the most demanding of circumstances. Dogs in herding trials are judged against a set of standards as well as other dogs.

Recognizing what your Rottweiler is trying to tell you is tantamount to being able to live harmoniously with your dog.

Behavior of Your Rottweiler

As a Rottweiler owner, you have selected your dog so that you and your loved ones can have a companion, a protector, a friend and a four-legged family member. You invest time, money and effort to care for and train the family's new charge. Of course, this chosen canine behaves perfectly! Well, perfectly *like a dog.*

THINK LIKE A DOG

Dogs do not think like humans, nor do humans think like dogs, though we try. Unfortunately, a dog is incapable of figuring out how humans think, so the responsibility falls on the owner to adopt a viable canine mindset. Dogs cannot rationalize and can only exist in the present moment. Many a dog owner makes the mistake in training of thinking that he can reprimand his dog for something the dog did a while ago. Basically, you cannot even reprimand a dog for something he did 20 seconds ago! Either catch

A dam with her puppies will act very protectively. Think of how a human mother might protect her child.

him in the act or forget it! It is a waste of your and your dog's time—in his mind, you are reprimanding him for whatever he is doing at that moment.

The following behavioral problems represent some which owners most commonly encounter. Every dog is unique and every situation is unique. No author could purport for you to solve your Rottweiler's problem simply by reading a chapter in a breed book. Here we outline some basic "dogspeak" so that owners' chances of solving behavioral problems are increased. Discuss bad habits with your vet and he can recommend a behavioral specialist to consult in appropriate cases. Since behavioral abnormalities are the leading reason for owners' abandoning their pets, we hope that you will make a valiant effort to solve your

Rottweilers must be exposed to other dogs when they are young so they will tolerate them when they are older.

TUG-OF-WAR
You should never play tug-of-war games with your puppy. Such games create a struggle for "top dog" position and teach the puppy that it is okay to challenge you. It will also encourage your puppy's natural tendency to bite down hard and *win*.

Rottweiler's problem. Patience and understanding are virtues that must dwell in every pet-loving household.

AGGRESSION

Aggression can be a very big problem in dogs, especially big dogs. Aggression, when not controlled, becomes dangerous. An aggressive dog, no matter the size, may lunge at, bite or even attack a person or another dog. Aggressive behavior is not to be tolerated. It is more than just inappropriate behavior; it is not safe, especially with a large, powerful breed such as the Rottweiler. It is painful for a family to watch its dog become unpredictable in his behavior to the point where they are afraid of the dog. And while not all aggressive behavior is dangerous, it can be frightening: growling, baring teeth, etc. It is important to get to the root of the problem to ascertain why the dog is acting in this manner. Aggression is a display of dominance, and the dog should not have the dominant role in his pack,

which is, in this case, your family.

It is important not to challenge an aggressive dog as this could provoke an attack. Observe your Rottweiler's body language. Does he make direct eye contact and stare? Does he try to make himself as large as possible: ears pricked, chest out, tail erect? Height and size signify authority in a dog pack—being taller or "above" another dog literally means that he is "above" in the social status. These body signals tell you that your Rottweiler

thinks he is in charge—a problem that needs to be dealt with. An aggressive dog is unpredictable in that you never know when he is going to strike and what he is going to do. You cannot understand why a dog that is playful and loving one minute is growling and snapping the next.

Fear is a common cause of aggression in dogs. If you can isolate what brings out the fear reaction, you can help the dog get over it. Supervise your Rottweiler's interactions with people and other dogs, and praise the dog when it goes well. If he starts to act aggressively in a situation, correct him and remove him from the situation. Do not let people approach the dog and start petting him without your express permission. That way, you can have the dog sit to accept petting, and praise him when he behaves properly. You are focusing on praise and on modifying his behavior by rewarding him when he acts appropriately. By being gentle and by supervising his interactions, you are showing him that there is no need to be afraid or defensive.

The best solution is to consult a behavioral specialist, one who has experience with the Rottweiler, if possible. Together, perhaps you can pinpoint the cause of your dog's aggression and do something about it. An aggressive dog cannot be trusted, and a dog that cannot be trusted is not safe to have as a family pet. If the pet Rottweiler becomes untrustworthy, he cannot be kept in the home with the family. The family must get rid of the dog. In the *very* worst case, the dog must be euthanized.

AGGRESSION TOWARD OTHER DOGS

A dog's aggressive behavior toward another dog stems from not enough exposure to other dogs at an early age. If other dogs make your Rottweiler nervous and agitated, he will lash out as a protective mechanism. A dog who has not received sufficient exposure to other canines tends to believe that he is the only dog on the planet. The animal becomes so dominant that he does not even show signs that he is fearful or

Dogs of all breeds can get along. Most dogs that grow up together become very accustomed to one another.

The Rottweiler's protective nature is instinctive and is passed on to the puppy through heredity.

tolerates the other dog. Keep this up until either he stops the aggressive behavior, learns to ignore the other dog or even accepts other dogs. Praise him lavishly for his correct behavior.

DOMINANT AGGRESSION

A social hierarchy is firmly established in a wild dog pack. The dog wants to dominate those under him and please those above him. Dogs know that there must be a leader. If you are not the obvious choice for emperor, the dog will assume the throne! These conflicting innate desires are what a dog owner is up against when he sets about training a dog. In training a dog to obey commands, the owner is reinforcing that he is the top dog in the "pack" and that the dog should, and should want

threatened. Without growling or any other physical signal as a warning, he will lunge at and bite the other dog. A way to correct this is to let your Rottweiler approach another dog when walking on lead. Watch very closely and at the very first sign of aggression, correct your Rottweiler and pull him away. Scold him for any sign of discomfort, and then praise him when he ignores or

to, serve his superior. Thus, the owner is suppressing the dog's urge to dominate by modifying his behavior and making him obedient.

An important part of training is taking every opportunity to reinforce that you are the leader. The simple action of making your Rottweiler sit to wait for his food instead of allowing him to run up to get it when he wants it says that you control when he eats; he is dependent on you for food. Although it may be difficult, do not give in to your dog's wishes every time he whines at you or looks at you with pleading eyes. It is a constant effort to show the dog that his place in the pack is at the bottom. This is not meant to sound cruel or inhumane. You love your Rottweiler and you should treat him with care and affection. You (hopefully) did not get a dog just so you could control another creature. Dog training is not about being cruel, it is about molding the dog's behavior into what is acceptable and teaching him to live by your rules. In theory, it is quite simple: catch him in appropriate behavior and reward him for it. Add a dog into the equation and it becomes a bit more trying, but as a rule of thumb, positive reinforcement is what works best.

With a dominant dog, punishment and negative reinforcement can have the opposite effect of what you are after. It can make a dog fearful and/or act out aggressively if he feels he is being challenged. Remember, a dominant dog perceives himself at the top of the social heap and will fight to defend his perceived status. The

FEAR IN A GROWN DOG

Fear in a grown dog is often the result of improper or incomplete socialization as a pup, or it can be the result of a traumatic experience he suffered when young. Keep in mind that the term "traumatic" is relative—something that you would not think twice about can leave a lasting negative impression on a puppy. If the dog experiences a similar experience later in life, he may try to fight back to protect himself. Again, this behavior is very unpredictable, especially if you do not know what is triggering his fear.

best way to prevent that is to never give him reason to think that he is in control in the first place. If you are having trouble training your Rottweiler and it seems as if he is constantly challenging your authority, seek the help of an obedience trainer or behavioral specialist. A professional will work with both you and your dog to teach you effective techniques to use at home. Beware of trainers who rely on excessively harsh methods; scolding is necessary now and then, but the focus in your training should *always* be on positive reinforcement.

NO KISSES

We all love our dogs and our dogs love us. They show their love and affection by licking us. This is not a very sanitary practice, as dogs lick and sniff in some unsavory places. Kissing your dog on the mouth is strictly forbidden, as parasites can be transmitted in this manner.

SEXUAL BEHAVIOR

Dogs exhibit certain sexual behaviors that may have influenced your choice of male or female when you first purchased your Rottweiler. Spaying/neutering will eliminate these behaviors, but if you are purchasing a dog that you wish to breed, you should be aware of what you will have to deal with throughout the dog's life.

Female dogs usually have two estruses per year, each season lasting about three weeks. These are the only times in which a female dog will mate, and she usually will not allow this until the second week of the cycle. If a bitch is not bred during the heat cycle, it is not uncommon for her to experience a false pregnancy, in which her mammary glands swell and she exhibits maternal tendencies toward toys or other objects.

With male dogs, owners must be aware that whole dogs (dogs who are not neutered) have the natural inclination to mark their territory. Males mark their territory by spraying small amounts of urine as they lift their legs in a macho ritual. Marking can occur both outdoors in the yard and around the neighborhood as well as indoors on furniture legs, curtains and the sofa. Such behavior can be very frustrating for the owner; early training is strongly urged before the "urge" strikes your dog. Neutering the male at

THE MIGHTY MALE

Males, whether castrated or not, will mount almost anything: a pillow, your leg or, much to your dismay, even your neighbor's leg. As with other types of inappropriate behavior, the dog must be corrected while in the act, which for once is not difficult. Often he will not let go! While a puppy is experimenting with his very first urges, his owners feel he needs to "sow his oats" and allow the pup to mount. As the pup grows into a full-size dog, with full-size urges, it becomes a nuisance and an embarrassment. Males always appear as if they are trying to "save the race," more determined and stronger than imaginable. While altering the dog at an appropriate age will limit the dog's desire, it usually does not remove it entirely.

an appropriate early age can solve this problem before it becomes a habit.

Other problems associated with males are wandering and mounting. Both of these habits, of course, belong to the unneutered dog, whose sexual drive leads him away from home in search of the bitch in heat. Males will mount females in heat, as well as any other dog, male or female, that happens to catch their fancy. Other possible mounting partners include his owner, the furniture, guests to the home and strangers on the street. Discourage such behavior early on.

Owners must further recognize that mounting is not merely a sexual expression but also one of dominance exhibited in males and females alike. Be consistent and persistent and you will find that you can "move mounters."

CHEWING

The national canine pastime is chewing! Every dog loves to sink his "canines" into a tasty bone, but sometimes that bone is attached to his owner's hand! Dogs need to chew, to massage their gums, to make their new teeth feel better and to exercise their jaws. This is a natural behavior deeply imbedded in all things canine. Your role as owner is not to stop chewing, but to redirect it to positive, chew-worthy objects. Be an informed owner and purchase proper chew toys for your Rottweiler, like strong nylon bones made for large dogs. Be sure that the devices are safe and durable, since your dog's safety is at risk. Again, the owner is responsible for ensuring a dog-proof environment. The best answer is prevention: that is, put your shoes, handbags and other tasty objects in their proper places (out of the reach of the growing canine mouth). Direct puppies to their toys whenever you see them tasting the furniture legs or the leg of your pants. Make a loud noise to attract the pup's attention and immediately escort him to his chew toy and engage him with the toy for at least four minutes, praising and encouraging him all the while.

JUMPING UP
Jumping up is a dog's friendly way of saying hello! Some dog owners do not mind when their dog jumps up, which is fine for them. The problem arises when guests come to the house and the dog greets them in the same manner—whether they like it or not! However friendly the greeting may be, chances are your visitors will not appreciate nearly being knocked over by 100 pounds of Rottweiler. The dog will not be able to distinguish upon whom he can jump and whom he cannot. Therefore, it is probably best to discourage this behavior entirely.

Pick a command such as "Off" (avoid using "Down" since you will use that for the dog to lie down) and tell him "Off" when he jumps up. Place him on the ground on all fours and have him sit, praising him the whole time.

Always lavish him with praise and petting when he is in the sit position. That way you are still giving him a warm affectionate greeting, because you are as pleased to see him as he is to see you!

DIGGING
Digging, which is seen as a destructive behavior to humans, is actually quite a natural behavior in dogs. Whether or not your dog is one of the "earth dogs" (also known as terriers), his desire to dig can be irrepressible and most frustrating to his owners. When digging occurs in your yard, it is actually a normal behavior redirected into something the dog can do in his everyday life. For example, in the wild, a dog would be actively seeking food, making his own shelter, etc. He would be using his paws in a purposeful manner; he would be using them for his survival. Since you provide him with food and shelter, he has no need to use his paws for these purposes, and so the energy that he would be using manifests itself in the form of little holes all over your yard and flower beds.

Perhaps your dog is digging as a reaction to boredom—it is somewhat similar to someone eating a whole bag of chips in front of the TV—because they are there and there is not anything better to do! Basically, the answer is to provide

Dogs need to chew...even if it is on your toes! Since puppies have needle-sharp teeth, they can inflict a painful (though playful) bite.

DOG TALK

Deciphering your dog's barks is very similar to understanding a baby's cries: there is a different cry for eating, sleeping, potty needs, etc. Your dog talks to you not only through howls and groans but also through his body language. Baring teeth, staring and inflating the chest are all threatening gestures. If a dog greets you by licking his nose, turning his head or yawning, these are friendly, peacemaking gestures..

the dog with adequate play and exercise so that his mind and paws are occupied, and so that he feels as if he is doing something useful.

Of course, digging is easiest to control if it is stopped as soon as possible, but it is often hard to catch a dog in the act, especially if he is alone in the yard during the day. If your dog is a compulsive digger and is not easily

distracted by other activities, you can designate an area on your property where it is okay for him to dig. If you catch him digging in an off-limits area of the yard, immediately bring him to the approved area and praise him for digging there. Keep a close eye on him so that you can catch him, as that is the only way he is going to understand what is permitted and what is not. If you bring him to a hole he dug an hour ago and tell him "No," he will understand that you are not fond of holes, dirt or flowers. If you catch him while he is stifle-deep in your tulips, that is when he will get your message.

BARKING

Dogs cannot talk—oh, what they would say if they could! Instead, barking is a dog's way of "talking." It can be somewhat frustrating because it is not always easy to tell what a dog means by his

Rottweilers that get enough exercise are less prone to destructive behavior.

bark—is he excited, happy, frightened, angry? Whatever it is that the dog is trying to say, he should not be punished for barking. It is only when the barking becomes excessive, and when the excessive barking becomes a bad habit, does the behavior need to be modified. If an intruder came into your home in the middle of the night and the dog barked a warning, wouldn't you be pleased? You would probably deem your dog a hero, a wonderful guardian and protector of the home. On the other hand, if a friend drops by unexpectedly and rings the doorbell and is greeted with a sudden sharp bark, you would probably be annoyed at the dog. But isn't it just the same behavior? The dog does not know any better...unless he sees who is at the door and it is someone he is familiar with, he will bark as a means of vocalizing that his (and your) territory is being threatened. While your friend is not posing a threat, it is all the same to the dog. Barking is his means of letting you know that there is an intrusion, whether friend or foe, on your property. This type of barking is instinctive and should not be discouraged.

Excessive habitual barking, however, is a problem that should be corrected early on. As your Rottweiler grows up, you will be able to tell when his barking is purposeful and when it is for no reason. You will become able to

HE'S PROTECTING YOU

Barking is your dog's way of protecting you. If he barks at a stranger walking past your house, a moving car or a fleeing cat, he is merely exercising his responsibility to protect his pack (YOU) and territory from a perceived intruder. Since the "intruder" usually keeps going, the dog thinks his barking chased it away and he feels fulfilled. This behavior leads your overly vocal friend to believe that he is the "dog in charge."

distinguish your dog's different barks and with what they are associated. For example, the bark when someone comes to the door will be different from the bark when he is excited to see you. It is similar to a person's tone of voice, except that the dog has to rely totally on tone of voice because he does not have the benefit of using words. An incessant barker will be evident at an early age.

There are some things that encourage a dog to bark. For example, if your dog barks non-stop for a few minutes and you give him a treat to quiet him, he believes that you are rewarding him for barking. He will associate barking with getting a treat, and will keep doing it until he is rewarded.

FOOD STEALING
Is your dog devising ways of stealing food from your counter tops?

If so, you must answer the following questions: Is your Rottweiler hungry, or is he "constantly famished" like every other chow hound? Why is there food on the counter top? Face it, some dogs are more food-motivated than others; some dogs are totally obsessed by the smell of beef and can only think of their next meal. Food stealing is terrific fun and always yields a great reward—*food*, glorious food.

The owner's goal, therefore, is to make the "reward" less rewarding, even startling! Plant a shaker can (an empty tin can with coins inside) on the counter so that it catches your pooch offguard. There are other devices available that will surprise the dog when he is looking for a mid-afternoon snack. Such remote-control devices, though not the first choice of some trainers, allow the correction to come from the object instead of the owner. These devices are also useful to keep the snacking Rottie from napping on furniture that is forbidden.

BEGGING

Just like food stealing, begging is a favorite pastime of hungry puppies! With that same reward—*food!* Dogs quickly learn that their owners keep the "good food" for themselves, and that we humans do not dine on kibble alone. Begging is a conditioned response related to a specific stimulus, time and place. The sounds of the kitchen, cans and bottles opening, crinkling bags, the smell of food in preparation, etc., will excite the chow hound and soon the paws are in the air!

Here is the solution to stop-

A dog that begs at the dinner table can be quite a nuisance. Once you start feeding your Rottweiler from the table, he will interpret this as being rewarded for his behavior.

Never give in to a beggar. The only way to break the begging habit is to ignore it.

ping this behavior: Never give into a beggar! You are rewarding the dog for sitting pretty, jumping up, whining and rubbing his nose into you by giving him that glorious reward—food. By ignoring the dog, you will (eventually) force the behavior into extinction. Note that the behavior likely gets worse before it disappears, so be sure there are not any "softies" in the family who will give in to little "Oliver" every time he whimpers, "More, please."

SEPARATION ANXIETY

Puppies first experience separation anxiety, that is fear of being left alone, as soon as they are weaned and removed from their dam. This is a normal reaction, no different than the child who cries as his mom leaves him on the first day of school. Don't be like your sappy mom and cry right back—move on, and your Rottweiler puppy will suffer less in the long run.

Your Rottweiler may howl, whine or otherwise vocalize his displeasure at your leaving the house and his being left alone. This is a normal case of separation anxiety, but there are things that can be done to eliminate this problem. Your dog needs to learn that he will be fine on his own for a while and that he will not wither away if he is not attended to every minute of the day. In fact, constant attention can lead to separation anxiety in the first place. If you are endlessly coddling and cooing over your dog, he will come to expect this from you all of the time and it will be more traumatic for him when you are not there. Obviously, you enjoy spending time with your dog, and he thrives on your love and attention. However, it should not become a

SMILE!
Dogs and humans may be the only animals that smile. A dog will imitate the smile on his owner's face when he greets a friend. The dog only smiles at his human friends; he never smiles at another dog or a cat. Usually, a dog rolls up his lips and shows his teeth in a clenched mouth while rolling over onto his back, begging for a soft scratch.

"LONELY WOLF"

The number of dogs that suffer from separation anxiety is on the rise as more and more pet owners find themselves at work all day. New attention is being paid to this problem, which is especially hard to diagnose since it is only evident when the dog is alone. Research is currently being done to help educate dog owners about separation anxiety and how they can help minimize this problem in their dogs.

dependent relationship where he is heartbroken without you.

One thing you can do to minimize separation anxiety is to make your entrances and exits as low-key as possible. Do not give your dog a long drawn-out good-bye, and do not lavish him with hugs and kisses when you return. This is giving in to the attention that he craves, and it will only make him miss it more when you are away. Another thing you can try is to give your dog a treat when you leave; this will not only keep him occupied and keep his mind off the fact that you just left, but it will also help him associate your leaving with a good experience.

You may have to accustom your dog to being left alone in intervals, much like when you introduced your pup to his crate. Of course, when your dog starts whimpering as you approach the door, your first instinct will be to run to him and comfort him, but do not do it! Eventually he will adjust and be just fine if you take it in small steps. His anxiety stems from being placed in an unfamiliar situation; by familiarizing him with being alone, he will learn that he is okay. That is not to say you should purposely leave your dog home alone, but the dog needs to know that while he can depend on you for his care, you do not have to be by his side 24 hours a day.

When the dog is alone in the house, he should be confined to his crate or a designated dog-proof area of the house. This should be the area in which he sleeps, so he should already feel comfortable there and this should make him feel more at ease when he is alone. This is just one of the many times when the crate proves to be an invaluable tool for you and your dog, and another reinforcement of why your dog should view his crate as a happy place, a place of his own.

Leaving your pup alone can be easier if he has a familiar toy to keep him company when you are not with him.

COPROPHAGIA

Feces eating is, to most humans, one of the most disgusting behaviors that their dog could engage in, yet to the dog it is perfectly normal. It is hard for us to understand why a dog would want to eat his own feces; he could be seeking certain nutrients that are missing from his diet, he could be just plain hungry or he could be attracted by the pleasing (to a dog) scent. While coprophagia most often refers to the dog's eating his own feces, a dog may likely eat that of another animal as well if he comes across it. Dogs often find the stool of cats and horses more palatable than that of other dogs. Vets have found that diets with a low digestibility, containing relatively low levels of fiber and high levels of starch, increase coprophagia. Therefore, high-fiber diets may decrease the likelihood of dogs' eating feces. Both the consistency of the stool (how firm it feels in the dog's mouth) and the presence of undigested nutrients increase the likelihood. Once the dog develops diarrhea from feces eating, he will likely quit this distasteful habit, since dogs tend to prefer eating harder feces.

To discourage this behavior, first make sure that the food you are feeding your dog is nutritionally complete and that he is getting enough food. If changes in his diet do not seem to work, and

NO BUTTS ABOUT IT!
Dogs get to know each other by sniffing each other's backsides. It seems that each dog has a telltale odor, probably created by the anal glands. It also distinguishes sex and signals when a female will be receptive to a male's attention. Some dogs snap at another dog's intrusion of their private parts.

no medical cause can be found, you will have to modify the behavior through environmental control before it becomes a habit. There are some tricks you can try, such as adding an unpleasant-tasting substance to the feces to make them unpalatable or adding something to the dog's food that will make it unpleasant-tasting after it passes through the dog. The best way to prevent your dog from eating his stool is to make it unavailable—clean up after he eliminates and remove any stool from the yard.

Never reprimand the dog for stool eating, as this rarely impresses the dog. Vets recommend distracting the dog while he is in the act of stool eating. Coprophagia most frequently is seen in pups 6 to 12 months of age and usually disappears around the dog's first birthday.

GLOSSARY

This glossary is intended to help you, the Rottweiler owner, better understand the specific terms used in this book as well as other terms that might surface in discussions with your veterinarian during his care of your Rottweiler.

Abscess a pus-filled inflamed area of body tissue.

Acral lick granuloma unexplained licking of an area, usually the leg, that prevents healing of original wound.

Acute disease a disease whose onset is sudden and fast.

Albino an animal totally lacking in pigment (always white).

Allergy a known sensitivity that results from exposure to a given allergen.

Alopecia lack of hair.

Amaurosis an unexplained blindness from the retina.

Anemia red-blood-cell deficiency.

Arthritis joint inflammation.

Atopic dermatitis congenital-allergen-caused inflammation of the skin.

Atrophy wasting away caused by faulty nutrition; a reduction in size.

Bloat gastric dilatation.

Calculi mineral "stone" located in a vital organ, i.e., gall bladder.

Cancer a tumor that continues to expand and grow rapidly.

Carcinoma cancerous growth in the skin.

Cardiac arrhythmia irregular heartbeat.

Cardiomyopathy heart condition involving the septum and flow of blood.

Cartilage strong but pliable body tissue.

Cataract clouding of the eye lens.

Cherry eye third eyelid prolapsed gland.

Cleft palate improper growth of the two hard palates of the mouth.

Collie eye anomaly congenital defect of the back of the eye.

Congenital not the same as hereditary, but present at birth.

Congestive heart failure fluid buildup in lungs due to heart's inability to pump.

Conjunctivitis inflammation of the membrane that lines eyelids and eyeball.

Cow hocks poor rear legs that point inward; always incorrect.

Cryptorchid male animal with only one or both testicles undescended.

Cushing's disease condition caused by adrenal gland's producing too much corticosteroid.

Cyst uninflamed swelling containing non-pus-like fluid.

Degeneration deterioration of tissue.

Demodectic mange red-mite infestation caused by *Demodex canis*.

Dermatitis skin inflammation.

Dewclaw a functionless digit found on the inside of a dog's leg.

Diabetes insipidus disease of the hypothalamus gland, resulting in animal's passing great amounts of diluted urine.

Diabetes mellitus excess of glucose in bloodstream.

Distemper contagious viral disease of dogs that can be most deadly.

Distichiasis double layer of eyelashes on an eyelid.

Dysplasia abnormal, poor development of a body part, especially a joint.

Dystrophy inherited degeneration.

Eclampsia potentially deadly disease in post-partum bitches due to calcium deficiency.

Ectropion outward turning of the eyelid; opposite of entropion.

Eczema inflammatory skin disease, marked by itching.

Edema fluid accumulation in a specific area.

Entropion inward turning of the eyelid.

Epilepsy chronic disease of the nervous system characterized by seizures.

Exocrine pancreatic insufficiency body's inability to produce enough enzymes to aid digestion.

False pregnancy pseudo-pregnancy; bitch shows all signs of pregnancy but there is no fertilization.

Follicular mange demodectic mange.

Gastric dilatation bloat caused by the dog's swallowing air, resulting in distended, twisted stomach.

Gastroenteritis stomach or intestinal inflammation.

Gingivitis gum inflammation caused by plaque buildup.

Glaucoma increased eye pressure, affecting vision.

Heat stroke condition due to over-heating of an animal.

Hematemesis vomiting blood.

Hematoma blood-filled swollen area.

Hematuria blood in urine.

Hemophilia bleeding disorder due to lack of clotting factor.

Hemorrhage bleeding.

Heritable an inherited condition.

Hot spot moist eczema, characterized by dog's licking in same area.

Hyperglycemia excess glucose in blood.

Hypersensitivity allergy.

Hypertrophic cardiomyopathy left-ventricle septum becomes thickened and obstructs blood flow to heart.

Hypertrophic osteodystrophy condition affecting normal bone development.

Hypothyroidism disease caused by insufficient thyroid hormone.

Hypertrophy increased cell size, resulting in enlargement of organ.

Hypoglycemia glucose deficiency in blood.

Idiopathic disease of unknown cause.

IgA deficiency immunoglobin deficiency, resulting in digestive, breathing and skin problems.

Inbreeding mating two closely related animals, e.g., mother–son.

Inflammation the changes that occur to a tissue after injury, characterized by swelling, redness, pain, etc.

Jaundice yellow coloration of mucous membranes.

Keratoconjunctivitis sicca dry eye.

Leukemia malignant disease, characterized by white blood cells released into bloodstream.

Lick granuloma excessive licking of a wound, preventing proper healing.

Merle coat color that is diluted.

Monorchid a male animal with only one testicle descended.

Neuritis nerve inflammation.

Nicitating membrane third eyelid pulling across the eye.

Nodular dermatofibrosis lumps on toes and legs, usually associated with cancer of kidney and uterus.

Osteochondritis bone or cartilage inflammation.

Outcrossing mating two breed representatives from different families.

Pancreatitis pancreas inflammation.

Pannus chronic superficial keratitis, affecting pigment and blood vessels of cornea.

Panosteitis inflammation of leg bones, characterized by lameness.

Papilloma wart.

Patellar luxation slipped kneecap, common in small dogs.

Patent ductus arteriosus an open blood vessel between pulmonary artery and aorta.

Penetrance frequency in which a trait shows up in offspring of animals carrying that inheritable trait.

Periodontitis acute or chronic inflammation of tissue surround the tooth.

Pneumonia lung inflammation.

Progressive retinal atrophy congenital disease of retina, causing blindness.

Pruritis persistent itching.

Retinal atrophy thin retina.

Seborrhea dry scurf or excess oil deposits on the skin.

Stomatitis mouth inflammation.

Tumor solid or fluid-filled swelling, resulting from abnormal growth.

Uremia waste product buildup in blood due to disease of kidneys.

Uveitis inflammation of the iris.

Von Willebrand's disease hereditary bleeding disease.

Wall eye lack of color in the iris.

Weaning separating the dam from her dependent, nursing young.

Zoonosis animal disease communicable to humans.

INDEX

My Rottweiler

PUT YOUR PUPPY'S FIRST PICTURE HERE

Dog's Name _____

Date _____ Photographer _____